Strong Women

THE EXPERT GUIDE TO BUILDING SELF-EMPOWERMENT

Cherie Rickard

Cherie Rickard Enterprises

Baton Rouge, Louisiana

 AVAILABLE ON EBOOK

Cherie Rickard/Cherie Rickard Enterprises

info@cherierickard.com

Baton Rouge, Louisiana/70449

www.cherierickard.com

©2017 JF Book Designs

Ordering Information:

Quantity sales. Special discounts are available on quantity purchases by corporations, associations, and others. For details, contact the "Special Sales Department" at the EMAIL address above.

Strong Women/ Cherie Rickard. —1st ed.

ISBN 978-1507640975

Contents

Dedication

Thank you to my loyal and loving husband Wendell, my amazing children Kristina and Carson, my parents Larry and Glenna Rowland, my sister Carla and nephew Holden for your loving support and encouragement to write my heart out.

Loving thanks to all of my sweet friends for standing by me and supporting my love to empower others through my writing.

I dedicate this book in Loving Memory of my precious son Bryant Kite who gives me peace in my grief just remembering his beautiful smile and sweet hugs. Mommy's little angel forever.

Bryant Carlton Kite

6/5/90 – 7/12/07

Right now you may know exactly what you want from your job, your relationships, your life, even the goals you want to achieve, the people you want to meet and the skills you want to learn. You have the desire to improve your life. But there's something missing — confidence, self-esteem and independence and the truth is there are few factors that impact your life as much as these. Without it you remain stuck in a lack of motivation, fear and self-doubt, even as you long for change. But there is a solution.

You can learn skills and upgrade your entire life today! Communication and dealing with impossible people will no longer be a stumbling block for you. Many people want to grow in confidence, but they try to do it without a plan. And while most confidence books may make you temporarily feel good, they fail to give you concrete ways to grow. Build a better you with the tools needed to gain your life back and get organized once again!

.

—STEP INTO YOUR PURPOSE

CHAPTER 1

Reflection

W hen I was a little girl I always dreamed of being Miss USA one day. I started competing in pageants when I was 12-years old and although my mom was very supportive she was never the stage Mom you see today on Toddlers & Tiaras. She probably wished I had a less expensive dream. I am not sure when or how my dream derailed exactly but I do know I made way too many concessions in my life for boys. I married very young to a man I thought I was would live happily ever after with but that ended 12 years down the road and realistically ended emotionally about 7 years down the road. As women we are conditioned to be caregivers and caretakers and some of us do this with ease and others not so much.

We have both genetics, learned and formed habits that determine our outer and inner structure. I have learned over the years and with re-search that no matter how you think you are, there is always a better you lingering inside.

Women get bogged down daily with children, work, personal issues, relationships, marriage struggles, and friendships, family and have to balance it all and then make time for themselves. It's a struggle but can be done. When you have inner strength meaning confidence, self-esteem and the desire to be independent you have the tools you need to make anything happen. We have to be in the right frame of mind of course to make ourselves better. Nobody can tell you that you need to be tougher, or stand up for yourself or lose weight if you do not have the desire to get there. So where do you start if you have the desire? You must first break the emotional bad habits that make you miserable. The myth that is takes 21 days to form a new habit is simply a myth and there is not enough scientific proof to prove differently. So how long does it really take to build a new habit?

Phillippa Lally is a health psychology researcher at University College London. In a study published in the European Journal of Social Psychology, Lally and her research team decided to find out just how long it actually takes to form a habit.

The study examined the habits of 96 people over a 12-week period. Each person chose one new habit for the 12 weeks and reported each day on whether or not they did the behavior and how automatic the behavior felt.

Some people chose simple habits like "drinking a bottle of water with lunch." Others chose more difficult tasks like "running for 15 minutes before dinner." At the end of the 12 weeks, the researchers analyzed the data to determine how long it took each person to go from starting a new behavior to automatically doing it.

On average, it takes more than 2 months before a new behavior becomes automatic — 66 days to be exact. And how long it takes a new habit to form can vary widely depending on the behavior, the person, and their circumstances. In Lally's study, it took an average of 18 days to 254 days for people to form a new habit.

In other words, if you want to set your realistic expectations, the truth is that it will probably take you two months to eight months to build a new behavior into your life — not 21 days. Interestingly, the researchers also found that "missing one opportunity to perform the behavior did not materially affect the habit formation process." In other words, it doesn't matter if you mess up every now and then. Building better habits is not an all-or-nothing process.

Before you let this dishearten you, let me explain three reasons why this research is actually inspiring.

First, there is no reason to get down on yourself if you try something for a few weeks and it doesn't become a habit. It's supposed to take longer than that anyway! There is no need to judge yourself if you can't master a behavior in 21 short days.

Second, you don't have to be perfect all of the time. Slipping back into your old ways has no measurable impact on your long-term habits. Give yourself permission to make mistakes, and develop strategies for getting back on track and do not allow someone else to say, "See I told you so" when you slip back into an old habit.

And third, embracing longer timelines can help us realize that habits are a process and not an event or a marathon. All of the "21 Days" hype can make it really easy to think, "Oh, I'll just do this and it'll be done." But habits never work that way. You have to embrace the process and commit to change and improvements. Having an understanding from the beginning will make it easier to manage your expectations and commit to making small, incremental improvements — rather than pressuring yourself into thinking that you have to do it all at once.

At the end of the day, how long it takes to form a particular habit doesn't really matter that much. Whether it takes 50 days or 500 days, you have to put in the work either way. The only way to get to Day 500 is to start with Day 1. So forget about the number and focus on doing the work.

So what habits do you need to change?

It can be eating, drinking, cleaning or lack of, being a perfectionist and stressing out when it not perfect, procrastinating, standing up for yourself, unable to take a compliment, thinking poorly of yourself, being a doormat, staying on track with projects, talking on the phone too much, allowing others to dictate your life and direction, falling for the wrong men over and over, allowing your children to get over on you even when you know you should stick to your plan. I could go on and on but you know right now what you need to change and you either have the desire or you don't. If you have the desire to change your old habits and form new ones, then keep reading.

When you have inner strength meaning confidence, self-esteem and the desire to be independent you have the tools you need to make anything happen.- Cherie Rickard

CHAPTER 2

How Confidence Can Change Your Life

The first step towards confidence is to determine exactly where you're missing it and the beliefs and behaviors holding you back. Next, you need to deconstruct old ways of thinking and patterns that keep you bound to the status quo and prevent you from taking confident action. Finally, you need to develop new mindsets and skills to practice regularly in order to rebuild your confidence muscle and help you develop into the self-assured, pro-active, confident person you want to be. As you practice new thoughts and behaviors, you're actually creating new neural pathways in your brain, supporting your real-world efforts.

Whether you're lacking confidence in general, or simply need support in a particular area, the techniques taught in building confidence can improve your entire life. Confidence is such an important factor that it's been proven to increase one's yearly salary by thousands of dollars, improve your relationships, and supercharge your career trajectory. By committing to a confidence buff up, you're taking control of your destiny and positioning yourself for personal and professional success. Most of the limitations that keep us from confidence are illusions and limiting beliefs.

Once you learn to shatter those illusions and break through limiting beliefs, you'll be empowered to accomplish anything you set your mind to.

So how do you go from a lack or poor confidence level to a higher confidence level depends on you. Ask yourself what is holding you back right now from exerting confidence? Is it a fear of rejection? Do you need to overcome social fear? Do you feel you will be perceived as arrogant? Do you not trust your decisions? Building confidence starts with getting motivated, overcoming fear of rejection, being assertive, and then you can empower your life for success

We all have a level a fear when it comes to exercising our confidence, but why are some more confident than others? Some would say it's because they look good or their smart or they have everything going for them. This is a false assumption. How you think someone else sees you should never be your only perception of you, but instead how you feel about yourself. I know some of the most beautiful, successful people you could ever meet and the insecurities they possess would surprise most. Building confidence is just like any habit and takes time to build and most of all patience with yourself. You have to be able to laugh at yourself first and then when others laugh you can say, "I know that was funny and ridiculous so let me start over" with a big smile on your face. When you can laugh at your own mistakes it's so much easier when you feel you've made a social mishap or made a mistake at work. In a social setting you should try wearing the outfit you love but feel ridiculous in. When you see an outfit in a store and you think that's gorgeous but I would feel silly wearing it, ask yourself why. Why would you feel silly? Is it that you normally wouldn't wear that because someone else may think you look silly? The perception that someone else would think less of or look down on you is a bad habit.

Try going into a boutique instead where you can get shopping assistance and ask the owner or fashion expert for help. It may be easier to shop alone and have a stranger who's an expert give you advice on fashion and knows what looks good together rather than you trying to piece together something you don't feel good in or instead of wearing the same old thing over and over. Boutique owners are like having your own personal shopper and fashion assistant rather than department-store shopping all by yourself. After you build up a self-aware-ness of putting together an outfit, then you can transition back to de-partment-store shopping if you prefer.

An example of confidence building in your work would be to ask to take the lead on a particular project. If you have the fear of failure but the desire to succeed you can gather all the resources, you need to make it happen. I love to Google and research anything that makes me more aware, educated and find the truth. You can also 'You Tube' almost anything now from interview skills to rebuilding an en-gine. I will discuss Interview techniques in a later chapter.

Building confidence will empower you to be more assertive without being arrogant. Assertiveness is a very important means for com-municating your needs in a way that is fair to both yourself and to others. Unfortunately, for some insecure people, assertive people are sometimes threatening and it is easier for the insecure people to label the assertive ones as arrogant, selfish, or unhelpful when they receive the answer "no" or when the assertive draw clear boundaries. In par-ticular, those with manipulation, neediness, and trust problems can see assertive responses as undermining their own agendas and will seek to respond with negative critiques of an assertive person's be-havior. This is where it can get a little tricky for the newly assertive convert, but it's no reason to suddenly start worrying that you are ar-rogant!

Women struggle the most with Confidence and Assertive behavior because as a man your labeled 'STRONG' and women are labeled 'BITCH'. Sorry, but I write honestly.

Try Some of These Assertiveness Steps when Building Confidence:

Don't- Look down or fidget

Do- Have good posture and eye contact

Don't-Let your voice shake or crack

Do-Take a deep breath and speak confidently

Don't- Speak too fast or quietly

Do-Speak slowly and loud enough to be heard

Don't- Let people brush you off

Do- Ask for their attention if they aren't giving it

Don't- Ramble

Do- Make your point and state your request

Don't- Look shabby

Do- Look clean and put together

Don't- Keep going on about the issue

Do- Stop once the problem is corrected

Don't- Be vague or wishy-washy

Do- Know what it is you want and state that

Don't- Misdirect the blame

Do- Address the policy or issue itself

Don't- Be aggressive

Do- Remain calm and collected

Don't- Remain silent

Do- Speak up if something's important to you

Don't- Be a doormat

Do- Have an opinion and don't be afraid to voice it

Don't- Yell

Do- Treat the other person with respect at all times

Remember changing your old habits takes time but practice makes perfect. When you try the same thing over and over and want a different result, try something different. There are certain situations we can all relate to that make us uneasy or leave us feeling we wish we had acted differently. I know seeing someone get bullied by a friend emotionally and then watching her walk away when she should've stood up for herself is frustrating. You may think, "Why didn't I say something or why didn't I say that?" Try a few tips when you're faced with certain situations.

Situation- The waiter forgets to place your order and your party waits 45 minutes for your food and they are rude about your frustration.

Response- Ask to speak with the manager and explain that you'd like your meal discounted or a free dessert.

Situation- The hem of your new paints comes undone during the first washing.

Response-Take it back to the store and request an exchange for a pair that won't unravel.

Situation- A neighbor's dog barks incessantly at all hours of the day and night and your neighbor lets this go on night after night.

Response- Tell him or her you'd like for them to find a way to silence the dog or at least bring it inside at night.

Situation- Someone cuts in line in front of you at the store checkout.

Response- I'm sorry, excuse me but I was next.

Situation- Someone makes an inappropriate comment that offends or insults you.

Response- Explain how what they said made you feel instead of holding a grudge.

Situation- Your friend suggests a restaurant, which you hate, numerous times for lunch in a row.

Response- Suggest another place you'd like to go instead and point out that the other place isn't your favorite.

Situation- Someone who was supposed to pay you back or do you a favor and forgot about it.

Response- Mention that you know they were probably just busy and failed to think about it, but you really do (fill in the blank).

Situation- A customer service rep is not willing to assist you in solving your issue.

Response- Ask specifically what the company policy is on the issue and whether they or a manager can approve an exception, if necessary.

Situation- You only hear from a friend when they need something and you are tired of it.

Response- Bring it to their attention. Chances are they either don't realize it.

Situation- Your boss or co-worker seems to take all the credit whenever a project is complete.

Response- Let them know the work was a team effort and you feel credit should be shared in all fairness.

Situation- You make plans with a friend and she cancels over and over.

Response- Tell her your time is also important and you can both get together when she makes time and plans for you both.

Situation- You feel you may have said something hurtful.

Response- Own up to your mistake immediately and apologize.

Situation- Someone cuts you off in traffic and almost causes an accident.

Response- Unless an accident occurred or you need the police, go on about your day. The person who cut you off isn't concerned. Keep your joy!

Situation- Your family member is embarrassing and you don't want to invite them to an event.

Response- If it's your event, then don't. You should never allow someone else to pressure you into something you don't feel good about.

Situation- It's your turn to make a speech and you your nerves are getting the best of you.

Response- Unless you are going to pass out, just make the speech. Confidence building is tackling your fears.

Situation- You want to apply for a job but don't know if you're qualified.

Response- Ask in advance position qualifications. Some companies have strict rules on hiring. If you think you're qualified, go for it and do your homework before the interview.

Part of building confidence is knowing how to negotiate a consensus rather than giving in to others decisions when you do not agree. Meeting in the middle and making a decision based on facts and understanding is better than throwing in the towel when things don't go your way.

How to reach a consensus is sometimes difficult for the type "A" personalities? Consensus is defined as "an opinion or position reached by a group as a whole" by the American Heritage Dictionary. Consensus decision-making is the process used to generate widespread agreement with two or more people. These instructions will guide you through that process.

There are 5 requirements of understanding

consensus decision-making:

1. Inclusion- With three or more people you must include all input in decision making. Nobody should be excluded or left out (unless they ask to be excluded).

2. Participation- Whether you're involved in a group decision or it's one with your significant other, friends, family or co-worker, you can

be a strong woman in decision-making. Not only should every person be included, but each and every person is also expected to participate by contributing opinions and suggestions. While there are various roles that others may have, each person has an equal share (and stake) in the final decision.

3. Cooperation - All the people involved collaborate and build upon each other's concerns and suggestions to come up with a decision or solution that will satisfy everyone in the relationship or group, rather than just the majority (while the minority is ignored). This is particularly important in a relationship so resentment is not formed with one-sided decisions.

4. Egalitarianism- Nobody's input is weighed more or less than anyone else's. Each has equal opportunity to amend, veto, or block ideas in a group setting. In a relationship, each person should be able to have input uninterrupted.

5. Resolution- An effective decision-making discussion works towards a common solution, despite differences because all perspectives in the group are taken into account. Through collaborating rather than competing, everyone is able to build closer relationships through the process. Resentment and rivalry between winners and losers is minimized.

You will be viewed as a strong woman with good communication skills when an agreement is achieved and everyone has participated in the process.

CHAPTER 3

Boosting Confidence
with Body Language

Our actual words are only partially what we say to one another in a conversation — the majority of what we express and communicate combines with what comes out of our mouth through our tone of voice, facial expressions, and body language. It's extremely common to have others immediately interpret your non-verbal cues and gestures. Learn to speak with confidence by being conscious of your body language and controlling it in your conversations. Surprisingly enough, when your body, face, and voice appear confident you will not only increase your actual self-confidence but the confidence others have in you will also increase.

I teach beauty contestants how their body language can easily affect their score, especially in the interview category. This is also true for anyone and it occurs every day in how others perceive you. You can't just walk through life acting as if you have no purpose. You should walk holding your head high and move your shoulders back. Keep your arms loose and your back straight. You can't always be in a hurry as if you're running someone's coffee errand, but instead lose the nerves and slow down a bit. Take your time and feel confident in your pace, and then your confidence will show.

As you pass another person and you catch someone's eye, always smile. It is difficult to fake a smile that is supposed to be genuine. A genuine-looking smile begins with the eyes: if you fake it you will appear to be disengaged. Be sure to let your teeth show and make eye contact when you smile. Eye contact should be maintained for at least a second.

When you meet another person's gaze you seem self-assured and confident. Someone that looks away as soon as another makes eye contact conveys that she is shy, untrustworthy and/or hurried.

Speak loudly and clearly. "Loudly" doesn't mean you should yell when talking; rather it means you should not inhibit your natural volume. Speak with clarity in your words and do not rush.

When you are standing or sitting, keep your body relaxed and loose. Do not tense your shoulders or cross your arms or legs, this will tell someone you are uninterested or guarded in the conversation. This is very important in interviews as well. Maintain good posture: nothing says confidence like a straight back and chin forward.

Start your day with positive "I am's" - I am talented, I am strong, I am healthy, I am smart, I am............. When you begin to speak positive about yourself you will begin to believe it. How we feel about ourselves on the inside shows on the outside. How can someone else feel good about you if you don't! Begin to tell yourself what you want to be and how you want to feel. If you're not feeling well most of the time, begin every single morning by saying, "I am healthy." Self-confidence starts on the inside and grows mentally before it shows outwardly.

CHAPTER 4

Overcome Low Self-Esteem

If you had a pill that would make you have the highest self-esteem you needed to become successful, would you take it? This book can only offer proven cognitive techniques for talking back to your self-critical voice, but you have to be willing to put in the work. You must learn how to handle your mistakes and respond well to criticism, foster compassion for yourself and others and set up goals that will enrich your life. Starting first with the visualization for self-acceptance will allow you to achieve your goals.

How do you feel inside every time you step out of the house? If it's a bright, cheery day you see outside your door, then go on and enjoy that sunshine. But if you are already complaining about the weather, then you know you need to maybe take a small peek into yourself. What does the weather have to do with self-esteem? Well, nothing! But the way you 'feel' about the things around you, and that includes the weather, says a lot about how you feel about yourself.

They say the material world is merely a reflection of how you feel inside. So if you can try to change the picture inside, it will be reflected on the outside too, quite naturally. With the right disposition, even rainy days can feel bright.

How to catch the negative critic in you: People are most often the hardest on themselves. Every time a negative or temporary life altering event on the outside happens, you begin to think about yourself as a loser and that everyone else as a great life. Stop that thought right there, catch it. Failures will cease to make you feel bad about yourself when you realize that they are only opportunities and not mighty hardships that God is trying to throw on you. Often, when something doesn't turn out the way you plan another opportunity comes to pass, we find it difficult to focus on what other opportunity could possibly be better and instead only focus on what did not happen.

After you master the skill of catching the critic (and you will become a master if you try for a few days), throw her out of your system and bring in a new, more sensible woman that you are. Even if you don't understand how to do this, it's fine. Just understand that the word 'critic' only connotes that your own mind is used to thinking and feeling bad all the time. To bring in the new woman means to simply start thinking good thoughts about you. Say for example, if after a failure at a competition or a business deal, you begin to think of yourself as a loser, just stop right there in your tracks, catch that thought, refuse to believe in it and replace it with an effective positive thought of a newer, bigger opportunity coming your way.

Stop comparing yourself to others: Though it's been said a million times already, it still holds true that every single individual on this planet is unique in their own way. What matters is not whether you are as good as the rest of the women, but whether you are good at being you and sharing your own gifts and talents with others. People have different lives and circumstances and they to have their successes and failures. You may think someone else has a better life because they have more money than you or a better husband or better friends, family or job. What you don't always know is the skeletons in their closet that we all have. You don't know what sacrifices they may have endured to have what they have and whether you would be willing to suffer such consequences. However, "skeletal" moments don't just have to do with only dark pasts. Skeletal moments can also be about embarrassing moments they have had that they simply feel too awful to speak of.

Respect yourself first: Love yourself more: Because if you don't respect yourself, then how can you expect others to respect you? Accept yourself, however you are at this moment, and that means physically and mentally. Physically, some of us are more endowed with good looks than others. Some of us have sharper minds than our peers, and that's perfectly fine. Whoever you are and however you are, there will always be something in you that absolutely nobody else will have. All you have to do is to find that out and proceed to work on improving it. I make no secret that I work on being healthy for 2-week intervals and then eat horrible and forget a gym exists. This is something I personally have to work on. We all have something we can work on to make us better. You may know right now that you are not such a great friend, work on being more dependable.

You have to allow for that reality that someone is going to make you feel bad: If somebody were to throw mud at you, would you just stand there and let it hit your head, hair or clothes or would you simply move aside and let it pass by you? The choice is yours. You cannot stop people from throwing stones and telling you all that they do, but you can choose to accept it and let it make you feel bad or to not accept it. Be very choosy and picky when it comes to taking advice from just anyone. Ask yourself if it makes sense and if it is helping you or if it's being given with alternative motives. If it's not helping you, then discard it. Associate with genuine, real positive people who will help you and feel good about yourself as a woman. See how the person giving advice lives her own life first. You wouldn't take nutritional advice from someone 80lbs overweight or medical advice from a non-clinician. You have your own best interest at heart so you'll do just fine!

Keeping a journal. I don't want to hear how you don't have time. With technology today you can write notes in your phone that is probably by your side most of the day. Write something good about yourself every day. Whenever you feel down and low in self-esteem, open up your journal to encourage yourself once again. For two times a day, once before bed and once after you've woken up, face the mirror and say three good things about yourself. If you cannot think of anything to say, enlist a trusting friend to send you a motivational text, tweet or Facebook post. Look up motivational quotes and tape to your computer at work or on your bathroom mirror.

Do unto others: Do one good thing to someone or something every day without expecting anything in return. It could be anything, from feeding a stray dog, giving a compliment to helping the elderly. When you can help someone else in their suffering or pain especially if it's a pain or situation you have been through you're actually healing yourself as well in return without realizing it. The feeling of having been helpful for another can be very uplifting.

Express your talents: Pick a hobby you are good at and become even better at it. Pride in something that you do helps to create a positive self-esteem. Examples of hobbies can be gardening, writing, blogging, embroidering, sewing or even wood refurnishing. It is hard to be down on yourself when you have created something physical and can look at it with pride and say to yourself "Look at what I have created".

The rich diversity in the world often helps us understand much more than we can ever expect to understand from any great books. If you have the privilege of travel you should take at least 1 trip each year that brings out the best in, you!

CHAPTER 5

How to Understand
Who You Are

Being someone else rather than yourself is life's hardest challenge sometimes.

Every person in the world is unique, meaning people differ according to their talent, abilities, body characteristics and many more unique features. Most people in this world don't think how to be themselves. They quite often try to become someone who they aren't. Now this is the place where problems arise.

The best way of understanding who you are is to identify and analyze the gifts you have been given such as abilities and talents. The most crucial point here is learning to understand your strengths and weaknesses. If you don't identify them when you are young, then that can lead to many problems in the beginning of your career life.

Don't try to be somebody who you aren't and don't ever get disappointed with who you are, because everyone in this world is unique. Sometimes you find yourself doing things and you have no idea why. Why did you yell at your son or daughter? Why did you choose to stay with your current job instead of taking a new one? Why did you argue with your spouse or parents about something you don't even care about? Our subconscious controls a huge amount of our behavior and the reasoning behind many of our decisions in life.

Our outwardly appearance can also play a huge role on how we think of ourselves on the inside. I am not saying you must be dressed up every second of the day but in many instances if you know how to look, you can gain a greater understanding of yourself, why you make the decisions that you do, what makes you happy, and how you might change for the better. (See chapter of empowering woman in fashion).

First, get an objective assessment. The first thing you can do to gain a greater understanding of yourself is to get someone to give you an objective assessment. Of course, you can ask people you know, but their experience of you will lead them to the same biases that you have. Getting some objective opinions will give you a more accurate picture and lead you to consider some things you might not even have thought of. There are a number of established tests that you can take to learn about the different aspects of yourself (and more than a few less-reputable ones).

The Myers-Briggs Personality type theory says that all people have 1 of 16 different basic personalities. These personalities can predict how you interact with people, the kinds of interpersonal problems and strengths that you have, and what kind of environment you live and work in best. A basic version of this test can be found online if you want to find out what you can learn from better understanding your personality.

If you're struggling to understand what makes you happy and what you should do with your life, consider taking a career test. These types of tests can help you decide what you might find the most satisfying, usually based on your personality and what you do for fun. There are lots of different ones available online, usually for free, but if you're in school you can probably get a more reputable one administered by your career counselor.

There is a theory that every person learns and processes their experience of the world in one of a number of different ways. This is called your "learning style". Knowing what learning style you have will help you even once you're out of school and can help you to understand why you struggle with some activities and excel at others. As with the others, there are a number of free tests that you can take online. Just be aware that this is a disputed science, with many theories about how many learning styles exist, and you may get different results depending on which test you take.

You can also find lots of other tests covering many subjects such as character writing exercises. When writers go to write a book, they will often do writing exercises that help them to better understand the characters that they're writing about. You can do these same exercises to get a better understanding of yourself and many can be found online for free. These exercises may not have anything official to say about you, often relying on you to draw your own conclusions about what your answers say about you, but they may lead you to think about things you never thought about before.

Try answering the following questions to get an idea of what this is like:

How would you describe yourself in one sentence?

What is your purpose in your life's story?

What is the most important thing that has ever happened to you?

How did it change you?

How are you different than the people around you?

Gain an understanding of who you are and what is most important to you by thinking about your strengths and weaknesses. Importantly, you'll want to compare your perception with your strengths and weaknesses to the strengths and weaknesses identified by your friends, family, and coworkers. The things that they see that you don't, can tell you a lot about yourself and how you see yourself.

My family sat in a restaurant one evening on Father's Day and played a fun game that my Mom had brought called "Roasted". My poor Daddy ended up being roasted. We always play a game when we all get together.

Game – Roasted:

Group must be a selection of individuals that know each other fairly well.

1. Select a person in the group to be roasted.

2. Select a game leader that will read questions.

3. The game leader writes down 6 questions of their choice in regards to the roasted player.

Ex: Describe the person being roasted in one word….

4. Each game participant writes down the answer about the one being roasted as the leader goes through 6 questions.

5. After all 6 questions are complete, each person tells the group what their answers are one by one about the one being roasted.

6. After complete, select another leader and one being roasted. Keep in mind this game can be really fun but can also bring to light what others perceive of you that you were not aware of.

It's important to know your strength and weaknesses so you know what aspects to work on and improve on and know how to use your strengths to help with conquering weaknesses.

Some examples of strengths include determination, devotion, self-discipline, thoughtfulness, decisiveness, patience, diplomacy, communication skills, and imagination or creativity.

Some examples of weaknesses include close-mindedness, self-centeredness, difficulty perceiving reality, judgment of others, and issues with control.

When determining attributes, you should also examine your priorities. What you think is most important in life and in your day-to-day interactions can tell you a lot about yourself. Think about your priorities, compare them to the priorities of other people you respect, and think what your conclusions say about you. Of course, you need to be open to the idea that you might not have your priorities in the best order (so many people don't), which can also teach you a lot about yourself.

If your house were burning down, what would you do? What would you save? This mind exercise does not work unless you're completely honest with yourself. It's amazing how fire exposes our priorities. Even if you'd save something practical, like your tax records, that still says something about you (probably that you prefer to be prepared and not meet resistance in life). If you save something like your Prada bag, that says a lot and obvious what it means.

Another way to tell what your priorities are is to imagine that someone you love was being openly criticized for something that you don't support (let's say, they're gay but you don't agree with the lifestyle). Do you support them? Protect them? How? What would you say? Our actions in the face of peer criticism can reveal our priorities and character.

Some examples of priorities that people often have include: money, family, sex, respect, security, stability, material possessions, and comfort.

You can also look at how you've changed over time. Look at your past and think about how what has happened to you over your lifetime and has it affected how you act and think today. Looking at how you've changed as a person can reveal a lot about why you act the way that you do, because our current behaviors are built on our past experiences. For example, maybe you tend to get really defensive around alcoholics or drug addicts and are very harsh to people you perceive as addicts. When you think about it, you might remember someone important to you or family member being addicted and how much pain this placed on the family growing up, which would explain you're stronger than normal reaction to that behavior from others now.

Check yourself when you experience strong emotions. Sometimes, you'll find yourself getting really angry, sad, happy, or excited. Understanding what sets off these stronger-than-normal reactions, what their root cause is, can help you understand yourself better.

For example, maybe you get really violently angry about people talking during a movie. Are you really angry about the talking or are you angry because you felt like it was a personal sign of disrespect towards you? Since this anger doesn't help the situation, you might be better off trying to find ways that you can be less concerned about people respecting you, just to keep your own blood pressure down. I am by no means condoning talking in a movie, this is a huge pet peeve of mine but you can let it go for a period of time and then politely ask the talking to stop if its distracting your ability to watch and hear the movie.

Watch out for repression and transference. Repression is when you don't want to think about something so you help yourself to forget it even happened. Example of this might be a friend that has wronged you in some way whether by betrayal or trust and you feel if you are going to remain friends then you should sweep it under the rug. The truth is that it's never swept under the rug and it will come back and attack you in some form. You need to recognize this behavior and address it with your friend immediately and then decide whether the friendship is worth saving.

Transference is when you emotionally react to one thing, but what you're really reacting to is something else. Both of these behaviors, which are very common, are unhealthy and finding out why you do them and finding ways to handle those emotions in a healthier way will make you a much happier person. For example, you might think that you're not sad about your grandma dying, but when your family decides to get rid of her favorite old chair you get really angry and upset. You're not really upset about the chair being gone. It was stained, smelled funny, and probably contained radioactive foam for all you know. You're upset that your grandma is gone. What's important is that you recognize this behavior and you address the real issues.

Notice how and when you talk about yourself. Do you turn every conversation you have into a conversation about yourself? Do you make jokes at your own expense whenever you talk about yourself? How and when you talk about yourself can reveal a lot about how you think and how you perceive yourself. It's healthy to talk about yourself sometimes and it's good to realize that you can't do everything, but you should pay attention to extremes and think about why you go to those extremes. For example, your friend might have just landed a big contract with work, but when you're all talking about it, you turn the conversation to be about you working on remodeling your home. This might be because you feel embarrassed that you have never had that type of deal or opportunity or maybe you don't work outside the home and feel inferior to your friend, so you want to make yourself feel busy, important or accomplished by making the conversation about you.

Look at how and why you interact with others. When you interact with people, do you tend to put them down? Do you make jokes at someone else's expense or casually make light of their new opportunity? Maybe you've noticed that you only choose to spend time with people that have more money than you or less money than you. Behaviors like this can also teach you things about yourself and what is really important to you. For example, if you're choosing to only spend time with friends that have more money than you, it may show that you want to feel wealthier by letting yourself pretend you're equal to your friends in that way. If you choose to associate with people that only have less money than you, it may show this is the only way you can feel superior to others.

Think about what you "hear" vs what was said. This is another thing you can look out for when examining your interactions with your friends and family. You might find that what you hear is something like "I need your help" when what they actually said was "I want your company", revealing that you have a strong need to feel useful to others. I often see a struggle in families when one person is the savior and the others depend on them. The role of savior can be exhausting and leaves little room for the savior to feel safe and comforted.

A fun and enlightening experiment can be to write your biography. Write your biography in 500 words in 20 minutes. This will require you to type very fast and think less about what you want to include and helping you to identify what your brain thinks is most important when defining who you are. For many people, 20 minutes won't even be enough time to type 500 words. Thinking about might be upsetting because you weren't able to get out on paper vs what you did say can also tell you things about yourself.

In today's society we want everything right now. The teenagers of today are far worse at demanding immediate gratification than I ever was. How long can you wait for gratification? Studies have shown that people who can delay satisfaction have a generally better time getting through life, getting better grades, more education, and maintaining a healthier body. Think about situations where you could have delayed gratification. What did you do? If you have trouble delaying on personal gratification, this is something to look out for and work on, since it often plays a role in your success. Stanford did a famous experiment with this called the Marshmallow Experiment, where they watched how some kids reacted when presented with marshmallow treats and then followed their progress through life, over the course of many decades. The children who put off their treat in favor of a bigger reward did better in school, work, and health-related areas vs those that insisted on their treat immediately.

In life we will be presented many challenges and being classified as a go-getter is earned. Analyze whether you need to tell or be told. When you're doing something, like work, think about whether you seek out your next task without having to be asked, whether you need someone else to tell you what to do before you act, or whether you'd rather skip all of that in favor of just telling someone else what to do. Each of these things can say different things about you, depending on the situation.

Remember that there's nothing wrong with needing someone to give you instructions and guidance before doing a task, especially something you have never attempted before. It's just something to be aware of so that you can better understand and control your own behavior when important things come up. For example, if you know you're bad at taking control in a situation but you know you really need to, you can think about how your reluctance is just "a habit" and merely a "comfort zone" tactic that you can break.

Look at the way you react in tough or new situations. When things get really tough, such as when you lose your job, you lose a friendship or spouse relationship, a loved one dies, or someone is threatening you, the more hidden or restrained parts of your character tend to come out. Think about how you've reacted in the past when the tension has gotten high. Why did you react the way that you did? How do you wish that you'd reacted? Would you be more likely to react that way now?

You can also imagine these scenarios, but be aware that your hypothetical responses may be clouded by your bias and not accurate to how you'd really react. Nobody wants to be labeled a push-over no more than you want to be called control freak but sometimes our core personality can outweigh what we actually feel we can do in a tough situation.

For example, imagine you were moving to a new town where no one knows you. Where would you go to make friends? What kind of people would you try to make friends with? Is there anything you'd change in terms of what you tell people about yourself vs what all your current friends know about you? This can reveal your priorities and what you're looking for in your social interactions. Some of you may even change your name but those are issues I will save for another book.

I want you to really think about how having power influences your behavior. If you're in any kind of position of power, you might want to think about the effect it has on your behavior. Power terminology can also mean wealth for the sake of behavior discussions. Many people, when put in a position of power, will become harsher, less open-minded, more controlling, and more suspicious.

When you find yourself making decisions that affect others, think about why you're really making those choices. Is it because it's the right thing to do or is it because you need to feel in-control of the situation? For example, when you're in charge of a group committee and you insist on placing all of your ideas into action. Does this really help and solve the issue at hand or are you just trying to find reasons to be right and in power of a situation?

Who and what influences us is can bring about success or failure.

Examine your influences. The things that have an influence on how you think and how you see the world can say a lot about you, whether you actually conform to what they teach or not. In seeing where your influences have shaped your behavior, you can better understand the root of the behaviors you do have. In seeing where you deviate from those taught behaviors, you can also identify your uniqueness and your own personal thinking. Some obvious things that could shape and influence you include media intake, such as TV shows, movies, books and magazines.

Also consider your parents, who might teach you things varying from tolerance vs racism to material wealth vs spiritual wealth.

Your friends, who will pressure you into enjoying certain things or introduce you to new and wonderful experiences. Who is in your life?

Do they bring any value or endless heartache and trouble? Toxic friendships can shape you for future friendships. Stand in good sound character, even if it means losing a few people in your life because this is a character trait of a strong woman.

Try to open yourself to reflection and let go of your defensiveness. If you want to really reflect and understand yourself better, you're going to need to think about parts of yourself that you really don't like and admit to some things you might not want to admit to. You'll be naturally defensive about admitting these kinds of things to yourself, but if you're really going to understand how you work, then you're going to need to let go of that defensiveness. Even if you don't let those barriers down for other people, you at least have to let them down for yourself. Becoming less defensive about your weaknesses can also mean opening yourself up to getting help from other people and making amends for past mistakes.

If you're more open to discussion, criticism, and change, then other people can really help you to understand and improve on yourself. Be honest with yourself. We lie to ourselves a lot more than we'd like to think about sometimes. We'll help ourselves to think that we made some questionable choices for noble or logical reasons, even when we were really just being vindictive or lazy. But hiding from the real reason behind our motives doesn't help us change and develop into better people. There's no point in lying to yourself. Even if you discover truths about yourself that you really don't like, this only give you the opportunity to face those problems head on instead of just pretending like they don't exist.

An example of self-denial would to actually be 50 lbs. over weight and tell yourself its water retention. If you retain 50lbs of water, you should seek medical attention immediately.

Listen to what others say to you and about you. Sometimes, especially when we do bad things, others will try and warn us against those behaviors. We also have a tendency not to listen. Sometimes this is good, because lots of people will say things about you just because they want to hurt you and their comment will have no basis in fact. But sometimes what they say is an honest, outsider's analysis of how you behave. Ask yourself if you trust the person that is critiquing you and if that answer is yes, then listen and put the guard down. There are haters in this world but if you're hearing the same statements over and over there may some validity to it.

Think about what people have said in the past and ask for some new opinions about your behavior. For example, your sister might notice that you tend to be a drama queen at times. However, this is unintentional on your part, which can serve to show you that your perception of reality is a bit off.

There's a big difference between evaluating what they say about you and letting that opinion control your life and actions. You shouldn't tailor your behavior to suit other people unless it is having a significantly negative impact on your life (and even then, you might want to consider that your environment might be the problem, not your behavior). Make changes because you want to change, not because someone else tells you that you should.

Giving advice will often give you a great opportunity to think through your own problems and reevaluate them from the outside. When looking at someone else's situation, you will be more likely to think about situations and circumstances that you never thought of before and how you would or should react to them.

You don't even have to do this activity for real, although helping your friends, family, and even strangers is a nice thing to do and I am a firm believer that when you help someone else heal you begin to heal you own wounds. Have you ever thought back and said, "Man, I wish I had that opportunity to do over again"? You can give advice to your past and future self, in the form of a letter. This will help you think through your past experiences and what you took away from them, as well as what is really important to you for the future. I believe taking the time to enjoy life and learn from your experiences is easier said than done because most people are never satisfied with what they have and where they are in life at this very moment. The best way to really get to know yourself, however, is to just experience life as it comes. Just like getting to know another person, understanding yourself takes time and you'll learn far more through experiencing life than by interviewing yourself and taking tests. You can try a few scenarios such as traveling. Traveling will put you in lots of different situations and test your ability to handle stress and adapt to change. You'll come to a greater understanding of your happiness, priorities, and dreams than you ever could just sitting in your same old boring life.

Try getting better educated in a particular subject. Education challenges us to think in new ways. Getting education will open your mind and lead you to think about things you'd never even considered before. Your interests and how you feel about these new things you learn can reveal things about you. Don't forget to first let go of expectations. Let go of other people's expectations for you. Let go of your expectations for yourself. Let go of your expectations for what life should be like. When you do this, you'll be more open to seeing what new experiences might make you happy and fulfilled. Life is a crazy rollercoaster and you're going to encounter a lot of things that scare you because they're new or different but don't close yourself to those experiences. They might make you happier than you've ever been.

CHAPTER 6

Are You Self-Absorbed?

We all want to think of ourselves as good people but the fact is not all people are equal in the character trait. Just as some are born with different eye color, we all have different personalities, experiences and circumstances that have molded us to what we are today.

Ask yourself, how much time do you spend considering the feelings of others? One classic sign of a self-absorbed person is the inability to put yourself in someone else's shoes. If you rarely spend time with your friends, colleagues, or family members without asking yourself how that person might be feeling, how your actions might affect that person, or how you would feel if the same upsetting or difficult situation the person is facing were on your plate, then you may be completely self-absorbed. It's okay to think about keeping yourself feeling positive, happy and content, but if you've almost never asked yourself how another person in your presence is feeling, then you may be in trouble.

Have you spent an entire evening with a friend without once caring about how he or she was feeling? That's not a good sign at all.

Have you offended people a number of times, and felt genuinely confused and surprised when you were called out on your actions? If you routinely upset people with your behavior and are pretty unaware of how you're making people feel a lot of the time, then you may be self-absorbed.

Do you get confused by the term "put yourself in someone else's shoes" or find it impossible to try to imagine or don't care to imagine what it might be like to be your co-worker, little sister, grandmother, or neighbor? You don't need to be able to perfectly imagine the interior lives of other people, but if you find it completely impossible to consider how they're feeling, then you may have a real problem.

See if you've spent a long time with someone who is upset without realizing it. Have you spent half an hour hanging out with someone on the brink of tears without noticing it because you were too busy talking about your latest date or purchase? Has someone close to you been passive-aggressively mad at you for something you did without you noticing the behavior until someone else pointed it out? Has your sister burst into tears right in front of you while you were examining your manicure, without you having the faintest idea why? If this is the case, then you may be too busy paying attention to your own feelings to care about how the people around you are feeling or going through.

Do you have a hard time telling the difference between a friend who is genuinely happy and a friend who says she's doing fine but who is secretly crying inside? Though some people are good at hiding their emotions, if you really have no sense of other people's moods because you're too busy thinking about your own, then you may be self-absorbed.

Have you found yourself going on and on about yourself while a friend is clearly too upset or distracted to listen? If this is the case, then it may be because you're not really paying attention to other people. See if you spend much of your social interactions wondering how you come off. Self-absorbed people tend to go into social interactions wanting to come off as interesting, charming, cute, or somehow exceptional. They rarely take the time to get to know the people they're talking to, to ask them real questions, or to even walk away with a handful of facts about a new person because they're so busy trying to promote themselves. If you've frequently found yourself walking away from a social interaction thinking that you did a great job of sounding smart, cool, or interesting without giving a second thought to the people you spoke to, then you may be self-absorbed.

Do you spend a lot of time rehashing what you said, how many times you made people laugh, or which people in a social situation were clearly attracted to you after you leave a conversation? If you think of this and little else, then you may be self-absorbed.

If you were having a conflict with a friend and were more worried about getting what you want, about coming off well, or about making sure the friend isn't mad at you than actually reaching a resolution, then you may be self-absorbed.

You're self-absorbed if, when you apologize to people, your main goal is make sure they still like you instead of showing how sorry you really are.

See if you spend time with people without wanting to get to know them. If you spend a lot of time around people but don't really think about their thoughts, goals, or fears, then it may be because you're looking more for an audience or a series of sidekicks than for deep connections with people. If you rarely ask other people about their hobbies, romantic interests, jobs, travels, childhood, or any other kinds of questions you may ask your "real friends," then it may be because you're self-absorbed.

Of course, some people are shy about asking other people about themselves, and that alone is not a sign that you're self-absorbed. However, if you don't even think of what goes on in other people's heads when you spend time with them, then you may be self-absorbed.

Think about a person you've spent a lot of time with in the last few months. Can you name ten key things about him or her? How about

twenty? If you're struggling
my jokes" or "He likes givi
a problem.

See if you're not open to co
who are self-absorbed tend
that any other feedback peo
and not useful. Of course, it
negative or to get you down
your co-workers, fellow stu
they are genuinely trying to
someone gives you construc
you she wishes you weren't
"That person's just trying to be mean to me, and his opinions are
worthless," then you may be self-absorbed.

This can be a particular problem in the workplace. If your boss or
colleagues have all mentioned the same thing, like that you need to
proofread your work or follow through on your ideas, and you always
brush them aside, then this may mean that you're so focused on the
fact that you always know what's best that you can't possibly imagine that someone else can help you improve as a person.

If one of your friends says something like, "I wish you'd listen to me
more," and your first response is to be defensive or angry, then you
may be too self-absorbed to really understand that your friend is trying to tell you something.

If people tend to tip toe around you because they're afraid of hurting
your feelings with a bit of honesty, then it may be because you're too
self-absorbed to really listen.

See if you often think other people are to blame when something goes
wrong. If something goes wrong, whether you've forgotten to pay the
bills at home or a project at work wasn't finished on time, your first
reaction shouldn't be that you've done everything perfectly while
everyone else around you has caused the problem to happen. If your

ⱴing doesn't go as planned, is to think
ⱴme for it, then it may be because you're

ⱴd people think they're the center of the universe. And
ⱴnter of the universe make a mistake?

See if you get bored or annoyed any time you're not the center of attention. Self-absorbed people tend to hate it when other people steal the spotlight, or when the focus of an event is simply not on them. If you get bored when you're at a concert because people are paying attention to the band and not you or bored when your friend is telling the story of her engagement to a group of people, then you may be self-absorbed. Self-absorbed people tend to think that whatever is happening to them is the most important thing out there, and they get impatient when the outside world suggests otherwise.

If you tend to get fidgety, check your phone, or look around the room, if one of your friends is telling a story that is more than five minutes long, then you may be self-absorbed.

If you find yourself getting annoyed when other people get praise or compliments because you think that you deserve them more, then it may be because you're self-absorbed.

See if you're always wanting or expecting praise. People who are self-absorbed tend to always be waiting for people to compliment them. If you not only love compliments but live for them, whether you want to be complimented on your new outfit, your smile, or even your ability to walk straight, then you may be self-absorbed. If you take a compliment as an unexpected delight or surprise, then that's normal, but if you feel that you're so great that you are absolutely owed a compliment just for breathing air, then you may be self-absorbed.

If you put on a new outfit and feel nearly shocked when other people don't tell you how good you look, then you may have a problem with thinking that other people are always thinking about you

See if you always feel like your problems are more important than anyone else's. People who are self-absorbed are unable to see past their own problems to consider the fact that other people may be suffering, too. If something bad happened to you, whether it's a break-up or an annoying conflict with your boss, and you can't seem to shut up about it to anyone within earshot without considering how those people might be feeling, then you may be self-absorbed. It's one thing to share your problems, but it's another to make your problems the most important part of all of your social interactions, no matter how much the people around you may be suffering.

If you're self-absorbed, then you may often compare your own problems to the problems of a friend who is trying to vent to you. If your friend just separated from her husband and your first impulse is to compare the relationship to your two-month relationship, then you may be self-absorbed.

If your friend is talking about a death in her family or some other awful experience, then your reaction should be to listen and to be there. If all you want to do is talk about how your grandmother died ten years ago or try to make it about yourself, then it may be because you're self-absorbed.

If you have a problem, whether it's a small argument at work or an altercation with a neighbor, and you feel like your ten best friends absolutely have to know every little detail, then it may be because you're self-absorbed.

See if you can't stand it when things aren't done your way. If you tend to take the attitude that it's your way or the highway, then it may be because you think that everything you think and do and feel is superior to what anyone else can come up with. Whether you're planning a project at work or organizing a dance at your school, if you think that you know exactly how to do things and hate it when other people take the reins, then it may be because you're self-absorbed. Self-absorbed people hate it when others take control because they like to be in power so that they can take all the credit.

If you find yourself feeling angry, annoyed, or even livid that someone else is trying to do things a different way, even if it's just a lab partner who has a new idea for how to conduct a simple experiment, then it may be because you're too self-absorbed to see any other options for getting a good grade or a co-worker getting praise for wrapping up an amazing project, then your natural reaction should be to be happy for the person. If you find yourself feeling jealous, angry, or confused about why you're not the one getting the credit whenever something good happens to someone else, then it may be because you're self-absorbed.

If someone is getting praise and you try to step up and even take the credit, then it's definitely a sign that you're self-absorbed.

See if you've rarely felt guilty or embarrassed about how you've acted. People who are self-absorbed tend not to care about hurting other people's feelings or coming off in a less-than-flattering light. They tend to think that everything they touch turns to gold and that they couldn't possibly do anything wrong. If you're the kind of person who gets totally drunk at her friend's wedding and thinks you don't need to apologize, or the kind of shows up an hour late to a dinner date and brushes it off, then it may be because you're self-absorbed.

If, when forced to apologize, you find yourself saying, "I'm sorry that you were hurt when I..." instead of owning up to your actions, then it may be because you really don't care about how you've treated people.

See if people you know have accused you of being self-absorbed. This one is a dead giveaway. It's one thing if your annoying sister once called you self-absorbed five years ago, and another if you keep hearing that you're self-absorbed from your co-workers, teachers, friends, parents, neighbors, Facebook friends, or pretty much everyone in your orbit. Of course, just because someone says something doesn't make it true, but if you've been accused of being selfish, self-absorbed, self-centered, or narcissistic by a number of people throughout your life, there may be some truth to it.

If you're really feeling ready to explore this possibility, then ask a close friend or family member for honest feedback. Say that you really want to improve yourself and that you aren't afraid of the truth.

See if you're known for forgetting birthdays, milestones, or other important events in others' lives. If you tend to routinely forget birthdays, high school graduations, promotions, or other important events in your friends' lives, then it may be because you're too focused on yourself to think about other people. Of course, we all get busy, but if you tend to forget birthdays and other important events fairly consistently, even when the friends whose life events you forget always tend to remember yours, then it may be because you're self-absorbed.

If you regularly forget birthdays and rarely apologize or follow up but then get really upset when other people forget your birthday, then you may be self-obsessed.

See if you avoid people who are outgoing or who command attention. People who are self-absorbed tend not to hang out with other people who are outgoing, loud, or who have lots of friends. They don't like competing for attention and would prefer it if the spotlight was on them and them alone. People who are self-absorbed hate standing by someone who is better-looking or more interesting than them, and seek out people who are mild-mannered or shy to have as sidekicks so they can always steal the show.

This can be true for your relationships as well. If you hate dating people who tend to steal the spotlight, it may be because you hate having the attention taken away from yourself.

See if you spend most of your social time talking about yourself. If you walk away from most social interactions with another person having talked about yourself 80% of the time, or walk away from a group situation having talked about yourself 50% of the time, then it may be because you're self-absorbed. If you're always talking about your work, what you did over the weekend, where you got your new purse, then it may be because you're so self-absorbed that you can't imagine other people would care about anything else.

See if you rarely ask people questions. If you've spent most of the social interaction talking and talking and haven't asked the other person or other people a single question about themselves, then you may be self-absorbed. If a simple "How are you?" or "How was your weekend?" is beyond you or you ask and interrupt while someone is in mid-sentence answering you then you may be self-absorbed.

See if you treat other people with the respect they deserve. People who are self-absorbed tend to be rude to other people because they don't think that they matter. If you're with short with the waitresses, flippant with people at work, or show up half an hour late to all of your dinner dates with your supposed best friend, then it may be because you think these people don't really deserve your time or attention.

Self-absorbed people are horrified when they themselves are mistreated, while routinely giving other people the cold shoulder without even recognizing it.

See if it's difficult for you to create deep relationships. If you have a lot of people you hang out with, but no one you really care about, no one you call crying at night, or no one who will be there when everything is a huge mess, then it may be because you're too focused on the superficial to really connect with people. People who are self-absorbed have superficial friends or acquaintances, but people don't really know them because they're too busy rambling on or promoting themselves to open themselves up to vulnerability or to show a side that is less than perfect. If you don't have someone you can call a real friend, then it may be because you're too focused on yourself to connect with others.

Of course, there are many reasons why people don't have deep friendships, such as being shy or afraid to open up to new people. However, if some of these other signs apply to you, then not having deep connections is another sign that you may be self-absorbed. This applies for friends as well as significant others. If you feel like you've dated a number of people but none of them have ever really gotten to know you and you've never really gotten to know them, then it may be because you're too focused on your image to take your relationship to a deeper level.

See if you rarely do something if it won't benefit you personally. If you're the kind of person who will only get to know someone because they can help you get a job, meet a cute guy, or up your social status, then it's because you're self-absorbed. If you tend to only hang out with people who you think are cool and who can give you something, whether it's a ride to school, work advice, or nice presents, then it's because you look at every social interaction only as a way to further your own goals. People who care about others take on friendships for the sake of the friendship itself, not for personal motivations.

It's not necessarily true that you would take on all of the traits and examples I have given you in order to be self-absorbed. You can be self-absorbed in one area of your life as well. You may just be someone who cares only what's in it for you and completely caring in some other area. The point of this chapter is to look inside, reflect conversations and what others have perceived of you and make a correct judgment on yourself. Improving you core emotionally with others is completely possible if you want to truly change or even recognize you have a problem at all.

BE GENUINE

Have you spent an entire evening with a friend without once caring about how he or she was feeling? That's not a good sign at all.

Think about a person you've spent a lot of time with in the last few months. Can you name ten key things about him or her?

www.CHERIERICKARD.com

CHAPTER 7

How to be a Spiritual Winner in Life

In life, there may be times when you lose yourself and feel out of control. It might be hard to feel like a winner when everything around you is causing you to feel like you're not. Simply following these tips will help you feel spiritually at peace with yourself and your surroundings.

Remember that in life, you're always a winner! As long as you follow your virtues, and live in your truth, you will be given beautiful gifts in return for simply going about your life. When you're positive, you're automatically in control.

Look your best every day! When you're dressed and looking good, you're prepared for the day and anything that may come your way. Being ready lets you be more decisive, and it lets you be spontaneous with your plans. Plus, it can boost confidence!

Make premonitions! They don't have to be all bad; in fact, let them all be positive. Do you feel a certain way? Then write down what you think may happen in the future, even if you feel it's out there.

Embrace your purpose! What do you feel is your spiritual purpose in life? Is it to be the backbone for everyone around you, or to help others? Whatever your purpose may be, live that purpose and never try to fight it! Live within the moments where you feel the happiest.

Be a neutral partner to life! Let life take you where life wants you to go, and end up where you are meant to be. Don't let false notions make you negative. Stay as neutral as you can in your daily affairs, because everything is subject to change. Just ride the wave.

Mentally liberate yourself! When people walk away, make sure you've uplifted them in some way. Whether that be making them happy, making them laugh, or giving them assistance, free them and do them a kind act.

Remember life's ultimate purpose! Some people are meant to be in your life so you can learn something beautiful, and begin a new chapter. Perhaps you will even be meant to stay with them for the rest of your life. When someone doesn't easily leave your life, think about it carefully. Perhaps they were meant to stay there.

Be Positive! Remember that in life, there is no 'good' or 'bad', per se. There is only life's will, and what is meant to be. Accept the bad in stride with the good, because it is all going to make you stronger, and bring you to a better place in the end.

Always stay positive!

Don't invest your happiness in others.

Stay true to yourself.

Follow your virtues and morals.

Live in your truth.

See beauty in everything.

Be a spiritual winner also mean being an inspiration to others. We gain acceptance and healing within ourselves when we accept others and help their healing. Becoming an inspirational person requires acknowledgment of your own talents, skills, and worth in this world. You will need to be someone who is willing to beat a path that may be rarely seen but you will shine the way and show others how things can be done, and usually for the better. Being inspirational is about speaking to other humans from your heart, so that no matter how many people you touch in your life, each of them will come away thinking about your verve for life, your energy, and your faith in their ability to be great too.

Being an inspiration begins within you, first you must inspire yourself to inspire others. Find something that makes you happy and do it. Remember that no one will care about what you do until you care! When you find that something that you love or happen to be very passionate about and care for it/take pride in it.

Even if you don't have a hobby or a talent that you know of, embrace your personality and be bold in the way you speak and carry yourself.

Be polite to everyone you come across.

Be helpful, if someone asks you a question about yourself or about what you do, then always do your best to answer.

Answer the question. Do this by:

Listening closely to the question.

Directly answering effectively and maybe even include your own personal additional advice.

Work hard. Never do half a job, because that's not inspirational at all. If you're going to attempt something, then do it to the best of your ability. When you're done be proud of yourself.

Carry yourself like a winner; Always smile and be happy and proud of   yourself.

Take on everything eagerly.

Don't ever give up anything.

Don't try to target one person to inspire, and don't try to inspire everyone individually. Just be the same inspiration to yourself and others day in and day out.

CHAPTER 8

Independence

B eing a strong, independent woman doesn't necessarily require that you be a die-hard feminist. Rather, it means learning to express who you are at your core, whether you are shy and soft-spoken or loud and assertive, without trying to fit a certain mold implied by you being a female. Learn how to undo this type of societal preconditioning and be the woman you are, whoever that may be. You may need to eliminate any negative social conditioning at the beginning.

Don't compare yourself to other women. While there is nothing wrong with having a female role model to look up to, constantly feeling jealous of other women will leave you feeling horrible about yourself. Though jealousy is natural to some degree, society tends to exacerbate female jealousy through advertisements and films that feature unrealistic standards of beauty. The result is a culture of women who feel insecure and unhappy with their own bodies.

The first step to overcoming jealousy is to recognize when you are actually experiencing it. If you find yourself reading a magazine or watching a commercial and comparing your own body to those of the models, take a moment to remind yourself that these women are paid to look the way they do. Their job is to maintain themselves under a certain weight and some of them lead very unhealthy lives to keep their figures. The cameras have special lighting and photos are touched so that these women who look "perfect" in magazines and in movies but usually look quite different in real life.

Try not to compare your own negative qualities with other women's positive qualities. Every woman has her own best assets, whether it is her breasts, her legs, her arms, her eyes, her hair, or her butt. Let go of trying to have it all, and appreciate what you do have. You can work on your negatives and be proud of your positives.

Don't base your happiness on being in a relationship. Having some-one to love should enhance your life and add value, not define it. No matter how bad you may think you need a relationship, you must first learn to love yourself before you can even begin to love somebody else. Remember that nothing usually lasts forever. Even the so-called perfect relationship might even end one day, so you need to be sure that you have a strong enough cushion to land on after a breakup or divorce. I don't just mean money when I say this. You need to have a strong mental and emotional mind as well. This is why you do not rely on someone else to make you happy.

If you are already in a relationship, be sure you have other things go-ing on in your life outside of the relationship, whether it is a hobby, committees, volunteer work, school, work, friends, a fitness routine, or your family.

It's important to protect your sexuality. Every woman, at one point or another, encounters a man who wants to take advantage of her sex-ually. It is important to learn both how and when to say no to a man who is making unwelcome advances on you.

If a man forces himself on you, then absolutely tell somebody imme-diately. It's never okay no matter what the circumstances. Don't be a victim or feel embarrassed. Don't let someone tell you that you may have brought it on yourself. Some have even gone so far as to claim that some women are "asking for it." Letting a man get away with a sexual crime teaches him that it is okay to do it again in the future. Report sexual harassment in the workplace or at school. Reporting these kinds of acts is not just for your own good; it could prevent the man from harassing other women in the future. There are other ways that men can take advantage of you sexually without forcing himself on you, so be aware of who you're in a relationship with. Do you find that he is always letting you pay? Is he another figurine in the household and does nothing really to help out but has all the energy in the world when its bedtime? Be careful you're not forming a co-dependent relationship around what is supposed to be a partnership.

Don't feel obligated to follow certain fashion trends. Being an independent woman means dressing the way you want, regardless of what people around you are telling you to wear. Use fashion as a way to express your mood, your taste, and your creativity. This does not mean it's okay to wear clothes that reveal private parts, a mid-drift that needs to be covered for the sake of others or tore and stained clothes. This means use the fashion and variety of designers to select what best suits you and your personality. Remember, that there's a reason why designers use 95-pound models on their runways: not everything that is on the cover of Vogue is figure-flattering. When deciding what to wear, you should take into account your body type first as well as your personal taste.

There's nothing wrong with being fashion-forward, but don't force yourself to keep up with trends that you don't like or that don't look good on you just because your friends wear it or like it. What looks good on your BFF may not look so hot on you and vice versa. If you enjoy keeping up with the trends, then learn how to make them work for you by putting your own personal spin on them and expressing yourself. (Tips later in the fashion chapter)

It's also important to just stay educated. Being educated not only gives you the skills and knowledge you will need to pursue your career, it also makes you well respected by the people you encounter in your life. Your level of education (whether formal or informal) reflects your intelligence and shows others that you care about things other than your own personal life. Not all education has to be attained through an institution such as a university. Keep up with current events in politics or know about the latest science and technology break through. Try reading books (both fiction and non-fiction), learn another language or watch documentaries. The history channel is not my favorite past time however when I do watch it, I always gain and retain information and feel educated on that subject. You may be a fashion expert and read all the latest updates on designers or have a high education of medical knowledge. No matter what it is, just know and learn something you can share with someone else and carry on a conversation as a knowledgeable person in that subject. It's just not okay to go through life with your head in the clouds and unable to carry on an adult conversation about a certain topic. Gossiping with your friends is not classified as an adult conversation for those of you that are walking around with their head in the clouds right now.

It's also so important today that women feel empowered to stand up for themselves whenever needed. Standing up for yourself as a woman and learning to fend for yourself in the real world is imperative if you want to avoid being taken advantage of by anyone. You must learn how to stand up for yourself at school, at work, and in your social life. If you over hear somebody making a sexist, racist, or otherwise disrespectful comment about you, don't let it slide. This doesn't necessarily mean engaging in an argument but yet calmly tell the person that what he or she said is not appreciated.

Let people know when they have wronged you. If somebody betrays you in any way, be sure to let him or her know. This will prevent the person from repeating the behavior in the future and they may think twice before doing it to someone else. Sometimes it only takes one time to call someone out, in order to shut them up.

Make sure your finances are not dependent on someone else. Mother's, raise your daughters to be loving and kind is so important but allowing them to depend on someone else to support them is doing them a grave injustice. If you're not teaching them in an early age to wash clothes and do chores while giving them an allowance to budget then you're setting them up to not only not know how to wash clothes but worse, have no idea how to make or manage money. You must know how to manage your finances. If you want to be truly independent, you must learn how to pay for your own life so that you don't have to rely on other people. Spending your money wisely, and avoiding wasteful or frivolous expenditures is a must, if you cannot afford what you're buying. If you're married and you rely on your husband to make and manage the money, then you may be setting yourself up for a huge failure down the road. It's okay to be a stay at home Mom, after you receive your education. It's okay that your husband works and you stay home raising children, as long as you would be able to transition into the work force if needed at any time. It's okay he manages the finances as long as you know what's coming in and what going out every month. Knowing your household income and evaluating your income by checking your bank statements regularly, and being sure to keep your own records as well so that you can catch errors is simply smart. When you're married it should be a team building exercise to manage finances. If you or your husband manage alone, then the other should ALWAYS be aware of what the budget is and live by it.

I am speaking to the younger generation of ladies who may be in college with this next statement. Prioritize your spending! Your top priorities should be on your basic necessities like food, shelter, and clothing. Things like expensive clothes, concerts, and vacations are luxuries in life. Learn how to differentiate between necessities and luxuries. Later in life when you earn enough money to spend a little more on these items I would tell you to live a little because you've earned it.

No matter what age or situation in life you can always give to others. One of the best ways you can exert your strength is to give back to those who are less fortunate than you. You don't have to be rich or affluent to make a positive impact in your community, you can start small. Consider volunteering at a non-profit organization in your community. Identify what issues you are most passionate about. The talents and skills you have and can share with someone else could be big or small. You can always volunteer at a soup kitchen, your local

SPCA, your church, your child's school or other community development program. You may be thinking you have nothing special to give and yet you're the best cook in your family. Maybe you could cook a meal once a month for a needy family. The churches and school social workers can always direct you towards a true needy family that would be so appreciative of your kindness. When you give of yourself, the feeling of contentment and pride within yourself give you a magical feeling that boost your confidence and feels your spirit with peace. Just start by practicing random acts of kindness. You don't have to become a formal volunteer to give back. If you see somebody in need, then simply help them. Even as small an act as helping somebody carry boxes can brighten up his or her day.

Your personal strength is manifested physically, mentally, spiritually and emotionally. If you want to be a strong, independent woman, you need to work hard in all four of those aspects of your life. We will all succeed in some areas better than others but, again, it's the negatives we work to improve on. Have self-love and respect for others. What we put out in the universe usually comes back. Karma! Just be aware of what you're putting out there. You may want to find a strong female role model to look up to that will give you the inspiration you need to feel more independent. This woman can be a family member, friend, spoke person, pastoral leader, female artist or politician.

CHAPTER 9

Communicating Effectively

Being a strong woman can be misunderstood to mean bossy or aggressive. Check that you are using assertive communication appropriately. If you are new to trying out assertiveness, or you're not feeling your usual self because of illness or stress, etc., you might be resorting to techniques that are more aggressive, passive aggressive, or making assumptions where there are none to be made, rather than being assertive with your communication. A quick check you can do is to think back through your comments and stance with the person in question and play back in your head what you said. Does it sound to you as if you were being assertive, or otherwise? Be honest with your own thoughts- it's about you!

Here's a good way to express yourself without being or coming across as arrogant. Sometimes factors come into the equation that shouldn't. Race, gender, married status, age, disabilities, illness, and so on can sometimes cause a person to assume that you have an "attitude", rather than an assertive style of communication. If you suspect that this is the situation, continue with your assertive communication and consider whether it is worth raising your concern that your status might be causing negative responses from the person accusing you of being arrogant, or whether this might even be something actionable in your workplace, committee, school, etc. environment. Good communication requires being an active listener. Letting people know your boundaries and feelings while at the same time allowing them space to talk, discuss, and open up about their feelings is important. Assertiveness is about give and take. You must take a little of their time to clarify your feelings and you give a lot of your time to hear about theirs. Remember that a good listener is also a flatterer and it's hard to find arrogance in that!

There will come a point in many situations and conversations and even debates that require you to be both humble and modest. Assertiveness and humility make a great combination. An assertive person doesn't need to shout "Me, me, me, look what I did!" from the rooftops. Assertive people are remembered because they stand firm in their needs, beliefs and interests are clear to others, and because they are reliable. They will frequently become a form of a role model for others seeking to assert themselves effectively. Take this role to heart but don't boast about it, big note yourself or become pushy, no matter how clever, popular, or successful you might be. Leave the boasting and referrals to those who have learned from you. It would be beneficial to reflect over your communications with others and your purpose. While assertiveness is about ensuring that others respect you and what you want in life, it ceases to be assertive communication when you use assertiveness techniques to confuse or outwit someone where you're more knowledgeable, cashed up, or better off than another person. Assertive communication is not about "getting your own way".

That's turning assertiveness into aggressive techniques of communication and that's when you'll be accused of being arrogant and bossy. Always think about the purpose of your communications. Will it make you better understood, will it ensure that your needs are fully communicated, and will it still respect the other person's need to be clearly understood and well informed? Try this example. Which of these examples do you prefer?

Hi, I'm "Arrogant". I bought this computer here last week. It's a real piece of junk. I can't get online half the time, it chewed up my hard drive, and it's loud and gives me a headache when I turn it on. Now I just know a new computer isn't supposed to behave this way but I suspect that your store is refurbishing old computers and selling them off as new ones. I mean, you guys think you're so smart but I'm one ahead of you and this really stinks. I mean, back in 1983 I practically invented the whole concept of refurbishing in my computer class but it was stolen from me, so nothing gets past me ever again. This is so serious and a breach of your store's customer service so I want the manager, not just a retail rep!"

Hi, I'm "Assertive". (Read their name badge) Hi Rita! I don't think we've met before; Jay took care of me when I came in before. Anyway, I bought this computer last week and it's a lemon. It doesn't connect properly to the internet no matter where I am, it chewed up my hard drive, and it seems to be louder than it should with a piercing noise that gives me a headache. Of course, a new computer isn't supposed to behave this way so I was hoping you might be able to look into having these issues fixed, or perhaps, even better, give me a new one to start over? I'd really like a new one because then I wouldn't have to worry it might fail on me again. I've always bought my gadgets from this store and I have always really appreciated your customer service. So Rita, do you think you might be able to help me out?"

In the first example, Arrogant starts off OK and then starts meandering, and ends up being aggressive. In the second example, Assertive keeps it light, considerate but still remains focused on the point, only she asks for help and buy-in from the retail assistant and doesn't disrespect her position. Note how she also called her by name from the start. Establishing rapport with someone for who they are, not just their role really matters and goes a long way as well as that is one incredible key to warding off people finding you arrogant when you are actually just practicing assertive communications. Remember the golden rule! You treat the other person like they matter and how you would want to be treated.

Assertive techniques take time to learn and nobody gets it right all the time. Apologizing is a good response to a failure to communicate assertively and there is always space to reopen that door to better communications.

Don't take negative comebacks to heart. When you are faced with one of life's more challenging personalities, the best thing to do is to not take it personally. Never allow someone who is joyless, steal your joy. Sometimes it is your self-assurance that is a cause of irritation in less secure people and their response is to try and project their evil way in through criticism. This is never a reason to fall back into old patterns of unhealthy communication. Stay firm and then reassert whatever your point is and choose to leave it there. It is something they can work on with the full enlightenment on where you stand.

There will be times when you're placed in a position of having to choose between differing viewpoints in a group, there might be accusations of arrogance against one division by the other. Always consider the possibility of being able to acknowledge both sides of the argument and finding the middle way to draw the concerns together for a resolution. You don't necessarily have to solve the situation but you can be a powerful facilitator to the group finding an answer to its division through your learned behaviors and assertive communications. In such situations, inform everyone that the situation is not one for blame, not one for recriminations, and not one for finding fault. Instead, help people to see that there is a chance for compromise by showing them where each has made assumptions about the other or the facts of the situation, while still upholding your own belief or opinion. And suggest that they have another look at things to reach a compromise. This will work in family disagreements, friendship tension and the work place. Because all perspectives in the group are taken into account. The resulting proposals are therefore able to address all the concerns affecting the decision as much as possible. This will in turn join or reunite a group, friends or family through collaboration rather than competing and build closer relationships through the process. Resentment and rivalry between winners and losers is then minimized. When an agreement is achieved and everyone has

participated in the process there is usually strong levels of cooperation in follow through. There are not likely to be disgruntled losers
who might undermine or passively sabotage others.

Whether you are speaking and communicating effectively in a work
environment, committee, friendship issue or family situation, you
need to decide how everyone will finalize a decision. A consensus
process allows others to generate as much agreement as possible. Often a super-majority is deemed sufficient. If your family for example
is unclear or fighting over belongings from grandpa, then how will
you reach a resolution where everyone is happy with the result? If
you're the assertive leader in the family or others consider your opinion over another, then this is your time to be the calming force. Some
use a simple majority vote or the judgment of the deemed leader in
the group. They can still use a consensus process to come up with
their opinion, regardless of how they finalize a decision. Hear from
John on why he feels he should get the gun collection and then from
Jane. If the family is willing to vote on who gets the guns, then let
them.

Participants are encouraged to think about the good of the whole
group as well as each other. This may mean accepting a popular vote
even if it is not your personal preference.

In consensus decision making everyone can voice their concerns during the discussion so that their ideas can be included. In the end,
however, they often will decide to accept the best effort of the family
rather than create friction or an "us against them" mentality. If you
are the one fighting for the guns, then remember to use your strong
woman communication skills whether you are a participant or helping delegate the group decision. You will be respected if you practice
what you preach.

With friends, you may need to test the waters before attempting a
lengthy discussion on why you believe Ann was in the wrong with a
disagreement involving another friend. Be careful not to involve
yourself as a strong woman in a situation that really is none of your

business. If you have an opinion about someone, it's usually best to keep that opinion to yourself rather than come across as a gossip. If you're venting or validating your opinion to a close friend or family member and are unsure if you were in the wrong or seeking another person's advice, then that's understandable. If it was a disagreement involving you directly, then discuss your concerns with the person your disgruntled with, hear her side and then reach a mutual boundary. Sometimes a solution is reached by finding a middle ground between both parties. Remember, to listen to each other.

CHAPTER 10

Tactics to Deal with Impossible People

ost people know someone who seems to make every situation toxic and impossible. Pointing out that these people are difficult and demanding won't get you anywhere, though because odds are, they don't even see they are a problem anyway. Whether a personality disorder or some other underlying issue causes the issue, you can learn how to navigate interactions with impossible people and preserve your own sanity. Like any conversation try to always to resist the urge to be defensive. Understand very clearly that you cannot beat these kinds of people, they're called "impossible" for a reason. In their minds, you are the source of all wrong doing, and nothing you can say is going to make them consider your side of the story. Your opinion is of no consequence, because you are already guilty, no matter what you do or say. At this point you are thinking about someone right now.

As much as you find it difficult and it goes against your very being, you have to just accept the situation. Impossible people do exist and there isn't a thing you can do about it. The first step is all about facing reality. If you think you might be dealing with an impossible person, you're probably right. When in doubt, proceed as instructed below. The headaches you save will be your own.

1. Do not call out the other person - Bluntly stating the problem will not improve your relationship with someone who is impossible. Instead of reaching reconciliation, he or she will likely just become more difficult. Recognize that you can't handle this like you would any other personal conflict — it's a special situation. This stands true for some ex-spouses as well. Chances are part of the issues when you were married were because reaching resolution was never possible.

Give up all hope of engaging these folks in any kind of reasonable conversation. It will never happen, at least not with you. Remember what happened in the course of the last fifty times you tried to have a civilized discussion about the status of your relationship with this person. Chances are, every such attempt ended in you being blamed for everything. Decide now to quit banging your head against a brick wall. Understand that it's not you, it's them. This can be surprisingly difficult, considering that impossible people have complete mastery of shifting the blame. Chances are, the more often they blame you, the more they themselves are actually at fault.

Keep in mind that this is not to be used as a way to blame them. Blaming is what impossible people do, and they do it well. Instead, you are only facing the facts, for your own sake.

That being said, here's a simple way to tell: if you accept responsibility for your own faults and resolve to improve yourself, it's probably not you. Remember, impossible people "can do no wrong."

Remember to "detach, disassociate and diffuse." When you're in the middle of a conflict with an impossible person, use the detach strategy.

2. Detach- Staying calm in the heat of the moment is paramount to your personal preservation and as a woman of strength it shows your

personal restraint. Spitting angry words, reacting with extreme emotions such as crying, will only stimulate them to do more of the difficult behavior.

Once you detach then you should disassociate yourself.

3. Disassociate- Remove yourself from the situation and treat it with indifference. Do not, under any circumstances bad talk, scream, lose control or resort to violence because then you are sinking down to their level. Add something positive by redirecting. Focus on something, anything, positive in the situation or in the conversation. Whatever you do just stay calm!

4. Diffuse- It can help to realize that the side of a conversation that contains the most truth will always come out, and it's best to "name the game" that an impossible person is playing, usually by asking them or the group a question that starts "Why...", you will move the conversation to a higher level, and the group, or even just the impossible individual, in a one-on-one will respond to this level of questioning. Although the individual may will respond by saying the "Why" is because of you.

5. Guard yourself against anger- If it helps, consider the fact that your anger is actually a precious gift to the impossible person. Anything you do or say while angry will be used against you over and over again. Impossible people tend to have amazing memories, and they will not hesitate to use a nearly endless laundry list of complaints from the past against you. Five years from now, you could be hearing about the angry remark you made today (which you didn't even mean in the first place). Impossible people will seize anything that provides them the opportunity to lay blame like it was gold.

6. Prepare for projection- Understand that you are going to be accused of much (or all) of their behavior yourself. If this impossible person gets a look at this section of my book, to them it will look like a page about you. Prepare yourself for the fact that the impossible person's flaws will always be attributed to you. In their minds, you

are at fault for everything. They will have an endless supply of arguments to support this, and if you make the mistake of encouraging them, they will be more than happy to tell you why you are the impossible person, and how ironic it is that you are under the mistaken impression that it is them.

7. Manage- Until it is over, your task in the relationship is to manage the impossible person, so that he or she deals less damage to you. As a manager, your best resources are silence (it really is golden in some cases such as this), humoring the other, and abandoning all hope of "fixing" the impossible person. Impossible people do not listen to reason. They can't (and even if they could, they wouldn't).

Recognize that you can't convince them that they have any responsibility for the problems between the two of you. They don't recognize (or if they did, wouldn't try to improve) their flaws for a very logical reason that they don't have any flaws according to them. You must understand and manage this mindset without casting blame and without giving in to anger. It's far easier said than done, and you will slip from time to time, but as time goes on, you'll become a better manager.

8. Consider that it might be a question of compatibility- Sometimes, a person who gets along with everybody else quite well is an impossible person for you personally. Most relationships between people contain many shades of gray, but some people simply mix as well as oil and water. It is common to hear your impossible person proclaim, "Everyone else likes me." This is an attempt to shift the blame to you, so don't buy it. It doesn't matter how this person interacts with others. The fact is, the way the two of you interact together is terrible. Blame never changes the facts.

9. Avoid getting cornered- Abstain from one-on-ones with this type of person. When you see them coming to corner you, suggest, and then demand that at least a third party be brought in. This will often

ward-off the impossible person's plans, and a typical response from them will be to unilaterally decide "we don't need anyone else." You are perfectly free to claim your need for a third party to help your understanding, and insist upon it. Bullies never stand up to a crowd.

10. Maintain your dignity and your self-esteem- If you have regular dealings with someone who tries to portray you as the source of all evil, you need to take active steps to maintain a positive self-image. Focus on the people who validate you. Realize that this person is hurting you on purpose to improve his or her self-image. When he or she comes out with a statement that is designed to hurt you, realize this; realize why he is saying that -- to get people to tell him that he's awesome. You are bigger and better than this person if you're not lowering yourself to this level. This person's opinion is not the truth nor does it define you. Understand that impossible people are particularly "fact-challenged."

If the attacks have little basis in raw fact, dismiss them. You can't possibly be as bad as this person would like you to believe you are. Do not defend yourself out loud, however. It will only provoke the impossible person into another tirade.

11. Part ways- Understand that eventually, you'll have to create a separation between yourself and an impossible person. Whether they are a friend, boss, co-worker, a family member, a parent, even a spouse, the time to leave will eventually manifest. Maintaining a relationship with an impossible person is, literally, impossible.

If you can't (or won't) make a physical departure immediately, make a mental one. In your mind, you've already left the relationship. The only thing left to do is wait for physical reality to reflect that fact.

More challenging is if this person is a spouse and you plan to stay with them. If you want to live with this person and spend the rest of your life this way, then you will have to recognize the places you cannot tread (i.e. the subjects that make the person impossible).

Avoid, as completely as possible, bringing up these subjects and keep to yourself. Find a truly wonderful hobby, and focus on it. If you are religious, focus on your religion. Educate yourself on this type of personality and read about narcissistic or bipolar personality disorders because this is a definite possibility. Even if it seems to you that they do not have NPD, read the articles about how to deal with them, because following the advice in the articles you find may help you.

Don't pick up bad habits. If you aren't careful, you could find yourself adopting much of the offender's own behavior, even if you aren't voluntarily trying. Issue blame entirely by understanding that this is just the way the other person is. These things define the impossible person's actions, and nothing you do can change any part of their past. If you have to live temporarily with this person and know eventually it will be time to leave, then be sure to protect your privacy. Impossible people will use any information on your personal life however small as a trump card against you. They can spin stories about you to other people (especially those close to you both) on a simple comment you made over lunch. Since they are specialists in manipulation, they are very good at making you talk.

Impossible people are good at seeming normal, and unless you are very convinced of who you are and where you stand in relation to the slight madness of this person, there will be times where you think "Hey, they are not so bad after all. I guess I could tell them what I am going through these days...." Big mistake! It will come back to you when you least expect it, in the dirtiest and manipulative way. If you have already deemed a co-worker impossible then things shared in confidence late night at the office between the two of you can be used in an ice cold analysis in front of the whole company. He/she will spare no information to prove to others how well they know you and they know what the best way to "handle" you are.

12. Be the opposite- Live as an example of tolerance, patience, humility, fairness and kindness. We are all influenced by the people in our environment — they don't have to be perfect all the time and neither do you. Give respect because you are human. If you don't receive respect, that's -sadly- their problem but always stand up for yourself in a calm cool manner when needed. Giving understanding will gain

understanding. Ultimately this sort of behavior is probably the only thing that might get through to them. They may not change in everything, but you can safely expect a change.

IMPORTANT TIPS:

Be detached from anything they say whether it's a compliment or criticism. If you give them power to build you up, then you also give them power to knock you down. Develop a sense of self-worth from within.

When the impossible person is abusing or slandering you, other people will start to show sympathy towards you. You don't need to do anything to make them look bad; she/he just digs his/her grave with no help from you. If they make you angry, others are also likely to be annoyed and your points may be devalued.

If the person you're talking with is getting on your last nerve, take a breather. Remember, they might just want to get a rise out of you so show them that they have no effect on you. Count to ten silently if you need to, filter your thoughts and then state your views with confidence. Look them in the eye. If you look at the ground or over their shoulder, they will interpret this as weak. If the person is still being impossible, then just ignore them. That person will eventually back down if they notice that they're not aggravating you so just be the bigger person and walk away.

When they whisper something negative to you in public, just say out loud, "Do you really want to discuss this here?" Hopefully, this will discourage them from extending the negativity within earshot of others. Impossible people don't necessarily want to bring on attention from everyone. In fact, the want everyone else to think you're the problem. Starting to sound familiar?

If you are in a position where you just can't leave, treat your situation like a game. Learn their strategy and develop counter strategies ahead of time. Just avoid taking them too far and becoming controlling yourself. Also know what the possible consequences there may be as a result of your actions so you can prepare for those too. If they still find a way to get to you, then don't feel bad. Just make a note of what happened and devise new strategies for that the next time. Eventually you'll find what works and what doesn't and you'll probably feel better as you realize you're 3 steps ahead outwitting them at every turn. Impossible people aren't so impossible when you can predict what they're going to say or do next. They'll just seem kind of sad. This works best on ex-spouses with children involved. The ultimate goal is to help free yourself mentally, not become their masters.

If you think that you are impossible, good job for realizing it! There may be hope for you yet. Learn to look at other people's opinions with an open mind. You are allowed to have your own, but recognize that just because an opinion is yours does not make it automatically right.

Note that the healthiest way to deal with an impossible person is to remove that person from your environment and life if you can. Do not torture yourself by exposing yourself to a destructive person when it's just not necessary.

A strong woman would not put up with it. You are worth more than that. Do not attempt to fix this person. That is not your responsibility and while you're working on them, you are not working on you. I have known women who cannot seem to let go of their ex-spouse's issues and faults. They are so use to working on them it becomes a habit form. You can forget about them even if you cannot avoid them. Stressing about them all of the time is the same as giving them your precious time when they don't even care about you. Do other activities and make new friends, go on a date, get a new job if it's a co-worker. That way you aren't wasting precious time by thinking about them constantly.

When you make your escape from the impossible person stay away. Don't ever go back once you break away no matter how much you love them or they say they've changed.

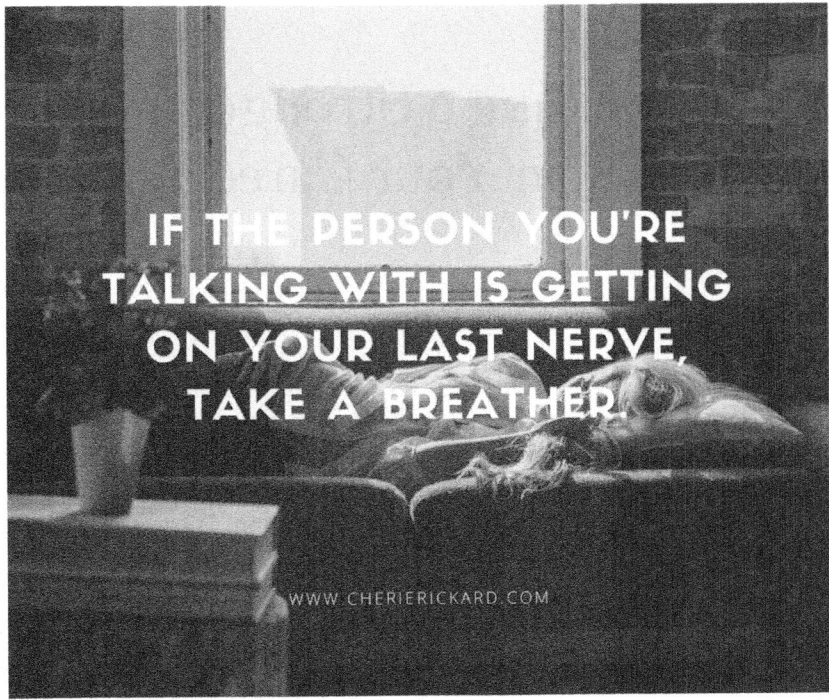

IF THE PERSON YOU'RE TALKING WITH IS GETTING ON YOUR LAST NERVE, TAKE A BREATHER.

WWW.CHERIERICKARD.COM

CHAPTER 11

Building a Stronger You in Your Career

Maybe you're feeling stuck in your job. Maybe you think your talents would be better served in a different career field. You may have been out of the work force for some time and don't know how to get back or have never worked outside the home and now not working is not an option. Whatever it is, it may be now is the time for a career makeover.

And if you decide it's time to take your career in a different direction, you won't be alone. The U.S. Bureau of Labor Statistics says that Baby Boomers changed jobs an average of 11 times between ages 18 and 44 (www.bls.gov).

Keep in mind that a career transition takes time. After all, how many years did you prepare for your current or most recent job? Give yourself the benefit of thoughtful planning, using a Desire, Discover, DO process to move forward.

Step 1: Desire! Your success depends upon knowing what you want and being ready to achieve it. If you are not sure yet what you want to do, try search engines to look up different careers, ask a trusted friend or family member their opinion. Being clear and energized about your goals gives you the drive to go back to school, take that continuing education course, find a mentor at work, or develop a business plan for your own entrepreneurial venture.

Before you make the leap, spend time thinking about what you do best, and how your unique set of skills and experiences can fill a need for an organization. Pull out your résumé and see how well it matches up with your goals. Ask a successful woman about how she made the most out of her success. Ask a successful friend if you can look at her resume as a template. Imagine your name on a business card. What's the title? What's the company or organization? What is your new work environment like? Scanning the want ads can help you think of possibilities. Once you've decided where you want to go, you're halfway there.

Step 2: Discover! You've set your goal. Now it's time to research the job market. Prioritize your new career must-haves: salary range, benefits, work environment, leadership level, etc. Considering how strongly you desire a career change, you may decide you are willing to move to a new town, cut your hair and cover the tattoos, or go back to school. Don't discount part-time, temporary, or freelance "consultant" positions. This can give you immediate experience and contacts. If you work full-time already, try out your dream side business in small doses on weekends or whenever you're off to see if it's going to be worth all of your efforts. Check out the jobs page on Websites of your target organizations, and then find someone inside who is willing to help you. This requires having the guts to make phone calls to strangers. Script and plan your approach before you make any calls, that's what the pros do. If you get discouraged, invest in a few hours of professional career counseling.

Step 3: DO! Make at least three phone calls every morning or on your break at work or whenever you have a few minutes. Get yourself invited to a chamber of commerce event or to a trade association meeting in a field you're investigating. If your desire is to break into the medical sales field I would make a few suggestions to help, considering this is my full-time line of work. Trade shows can be a great way to walk around and meet the most important people in a company, however be respectful of their time. They are not there to hire a new employee, they are there building relationships and selling to their current customers. You can ask anyone in the booth, who manages the sales team in your area and get an email. You can search MedReps.com as well for positions in your territory or an area you are willing to relocate to. It really helps if you know someone with in the industry you are willing to go to bat for you and your reputation. This is a very difficult field to break into to but once you're in, you're on your way! If your last interview was at the university job fair 30 years ago, you will need coaching and practice no matter what the job is— Look for committees that have public meeting in your area of interest, it's a great networking tool for experienced professionals and you can learn from them. Be coachable! If you are new to a role or position, then accept criticism from those experienced enough to educate you. If you're new career requires further education or skills training, find out what your options are and cost. In today's environment of high unemployment, there are more programs than ever to help you become qualified to do something new. You can purchase a program online or simply look for a You Tube video on whatever it is you need help with.

Look for a video coming soon from yours truly!

CHAPTER 12

6 Steps to the Power of Positive Thinking

W hen you set your mind on positive thoughts and strong positive beliefs then good things will begin to happen. I'm going to give you just 6 simple steps so that you can begin to get your mind focused on being more positive which will in turn attract more positive situations. When you do this you may have the power of positive thinking working for you. Whether you realize it or not your thoughts do have a direct impact on your life and those around you.

1. Write down every negative thought you have today. What is bothering you, who is bugging you and why is it haunting you? It's important to remember we become who we hang around and when we think positive you begin to attract positive people into your life and the kind of people who will help you succeed. Thoughts that you regularly think about end up creating beliefs and you begin to believe what you regularly think about. What you think about, focus on and thoughts that repeatedly run through your head soon become beliefs. It is these beliefs that your subconscious mind picks up on and sees as a blueprint. Your subconscious then follows the blueprint and creates your daily life based on these beliefs and thoughts.

2. Take each negative thought on your list and replace it with a positive thought that outweighs the negative thought such as your talent, positive trait, person in your life, successes you have had, people who have had a positive effect on your life…. etc. The power of positive thinking is directly connected to your ability to remove, control or eliminate negative thoughts. Keeping thoughts of fear, worry, doubt, pain, sorrow and hopeless outcomes will eventually destroy your life. When we have a tragic blow in life we have to remember it's not the blow that defines your future, it's how we use that blow and transform it into good. Good for us and /or someone else. If you're not happy with your life, if things aren't going the way you want, then simply track your thoughts and uncover your beliefs. Replacing a positive thought or talent for a negative thought listed will open our minds up to what is really on the fore front of our mind.

3. Focus on what it is you want out of life exactly. Don't change your mind day after day depending on the weather and what is easiest. If you want your real hopes and dreams to come to pass you must focus on them. Always remember our plans in life are not always God's plans for us, so keep in mind unanswered prayers are sometimes our biggest blessings in life. Ex: If you want to have a better career then focus on how to obtain that career, research how to gain insight into that career goal, join a career focus group, take a class or become certified in the field your seeking, see a counselor if you're a student, join social media groups and search for others that already show success in your future career and reach out to them as someone seeking a mentor. You will be surprised how people will help you when you approach them in a way of asking for guidance from an expert. Speak of your future career as "when I become (_____)" not if I become.

4. Surround yourself with positive successful people. I am not saying dump your friends and find new ones. I am saying pay attention to who you spend a majority of your time with. Success is not always measured by outcomes. You may know someone very successful and they are also self-centered, egotistical and self-nurturing individuals. This is NOT success. Success is doing what you love, feeling joyful, sharing your success and surrounding yourself with good genuine

people who you love and love you. Are your week days or weekends filled with others in your same rut or people that have gone out and gained success? If your mourning or grieving a tragic loss in your life do you find yourself allowing others to help you through your pain or latching onto people who are depressed and allow you to stay depressed? Ex: If your idea of success is to be happily married one day to the man or woman of your dreams and you spend weekends in the bar with your friends, then odds are against you! Ask the happily married couples you know how they met and how they keep their marriage on the right track. When your mind is filled with negative thoughts you end up attracting more of what and who you don't want.

5. Create a positive thinking pattern every day. When you wake up is your first thought negative or positive? Tomorrow morning, make a conscious effort to make a note of what your first thought is. Do this for 9 days and when your pattern begins to change for the positive you will be headed in the right direction. If you want to create a better life, if you want to enjoy greater success, happiness and enjoy more of the things you want, while getting rid of the negative aspects of your life then you have to eliminate the negative thinking and stop making excuses to keep negative thoughts.

6. Positive thinking is something you should practice every day and that means eliminating the negative thoughts every day. You do this by what brings you joy in life. Do you actively pursue what makes you happy or just talk about doing it someday? When you are all talk and no action we set ourselves up lacking credibility with others and our own thinking. Ex: "I am going back to school this fall" ...yet we never go. "I am going to find a good job doing what I love" .... yet we never even look. "I am going to get involved in school, church, projects etc." .... yet we never take the first step. Building credible thoughts through exercises, books, positive programs, daily devotionals, bible study, lunch groups, professional organizations and continuing education paves the way for success.

Surround yourself with who and what you love and turn your life's most tragic blows into triumph for yourself and for those around you!

POWER OF POSITIVE THINKING

YOU ARE WHO YOU THINK YOU ARE!

CHAPTER 13

Be a Strong Woman and Inspire

I f you need a Strong female role model these days all have to do is turn on the television or search the internet and see powerful woman like Oprah Winfrey who is a philanthropist, actress and all-round global presence. Oprah has endured and survived a tumultuous life, rising to become the most influential and powerful woman on television today, with her own hugely successful network and a worldwide following that stretches into millions. She also uses her network as a platform for improving the wellbeing of her viewers and strives to have a positive, meaningful effect in the world.

You certainly don't have to be Oprah to be classified as a strong woman. There are so many women working to create a difference and make their dreams come true. It all begins with the belief in yourself. If you don't believe in yourself, then how can you expect anyone else to? Women, for the most part can be fearless when it comes to changing the game and trying new things. Our level of tenacity is only matched by our level of passion. It's us emotionally strong women who motivate the rest to push on and who emerge as voices of change. However, honing in on your skills and making a name for yourself is not easy; you need the drive, and you need to not get in your own way. It truly takes kick-butt women to encourage future kick-butt women. I have the privilege of knowing and speaking with five go-getters — confident females who are leaders in their field and aren't afraid to take their passion and make it their reality.

Emotionally strong women first and foremost believe in themselves. If you look at all five women, one characteristic they all have in common is self-confidence. Meet these incredible ladies in chapters to come. Empowering Women in fashion, make-up artistry, nutrition and fitness.

CHAPTER 14

6 Characteristics of a Genuine Friend

We all have people in our life we consider friends but how well do you really know someone before you call them a friend? Do we use the word "friend" too loosely? We have many different relationships in our life and just because you know someone by way of a work, neighborhood, friend of a friend we tend to refer to them as our friends. How do you really know who is a genuine friend versus a phony friend? As hard as it may be to recognize at times it's important to know there isn't always sincerity that sits behind every smiling face. Today we live in such a competitive world where deceit is common so it's best to know who you are associating with. Unfortunately phony friends exist just as much, if not more, than real friends. Just as the Prada purse you can buy on the street behind the curtain in New York looks so much like the purse in the case at Saks, it takes closer inspection to actually see the difference. Like my Mom always said, "You will be able to count your real friends on one hand when you get older."

Tips to remember:

1. Real friends will ask you how you're doing because they really want to know. Phony friends are usually more concerned with their own needs than yours or anyone else's. It's okay to be self-aware but not self-centered. Phonies tend to ask you how you're doing and as you are in mid-sentence they may interrupt to start talking about themselves. They are not really listening to you, but waiting for a break in conversation to butt in and talk about themselves. Next time your "friend" does this, call them out on it. Ex: "I'm sorry to interrupt, I thought you asked me how I was doing and I was answering you"

2. Genuine friends will call you just to ask how you're doing, what you're doing or make plans with you for a fun outing. Phonies only call you when they want or need something and they are very unapologetic about it. If your friends can't deem you worthy of their time enough to talk to you other than when they need you then your question is easily answered. If you want to prove your on to them you could answer the phone and say, "Hey _____, what can I do for you today?" Chances are they are so self-absorbed they won't notice. You may have those phonies that make plans with you with no intentions of actually carrying them though. To me, these phonies are the worst kind.

3. You feel more comfortable and can be yourself anytime your real friends are around. I am a firm believer that nobody can make you feel inferior or make you feel a certain way unless you allow them to, however it's the gut feeling I am referring to when I say a fake friend leaves you with a feeling of emptiness and disconnect. You may even feel you have to act, dress or talk a certain way in order to be accepted. This is

a horrible feeling and chances are it's not you, it's them and your intuition is zoning in on negative energy. Remember money can only buy things, not class.

4. You always have a genuine hug, call or maybe a card when you achieve anything special or have congratulations in order from your real friends. They won't try to "one up" your every success. Real friends are supportive and they are constantly sharing positive words of encouragement. You win an award of excellence at work, or land a promotion, achieve a personal goal you have worked on for a long time. No matter what the scenario they will be there to pat you on your back and push you forward. Phonies are so opposite its plainly noticeable because they don't like any attention unless it's on them. They will hear of your success and try to pull the attention off of you and onto them in some way. They have competitive mentality with you and their other so called friends around them. When you share good news it should never get a response of "well guess what happen to me" reaction or embellishment of their story just to top your proud moment.

5. Real friends choose to protect your reputation at all cost. When you have a true friend they will never stand silent when someone is talking about you in a negative way or stirring up unnecessary gossip. A real friend doesn't ride the fence when someone isn't in your corner and then call it "I can't take sides." Standing up for a friend is not taking sides, it's called good character. Fake friends will join in on the lies or gossip or stand silent in opinion even when they know the truth. I am not saying start an argument or make anyone uncomfortable, I am saying when faced in that situation a true friend will stop it before it starts by saying "in _____ defense, she/he is not here to defend themselves or tell the story so we should save this conversation for another time." Short and sweet and impressive. You will be applauded by the group!

6. Just as a real friend is there for you in the good times, they are also there for you in the bad times. In one time or another we will all be

struck with a blow of tragedy in our life. You may be facing divorce, death of a loved-one, bankruptcy, terminal illness in your family, total loss in a fire or storm or even a job loss. The list goes on to what can and could happen to each of us with or without warning.

This is when a genuine friend is needed the most. If you are a real friend, then you know your friend better than anyone and you know what they need from you even if you have never faced what they are facing. This is not the time to disappear or make excuses. The phonies will shine brighter than stars during tragedy making your tragedy all about them for attention or simply walk away. When you go through tragedy, look around you and see who is there calling, bringing you what you need, caring for your needs, supporting you or listening with a shoulder to cry on.

Spotting a genuine friend is easy if we pay attention to who is around us. Watch their eye contact when you're talking to them. Do they see and hear you or are they looking around you to see who is in the room or waiting to talk about themselves? Their actions and body language will tell you more than what they say.

Friends are more than just good companions. They are influential people in your life. They can either have a negative or a positive influence. They are supportive, caring and loving even when there is indifference. Be the person you want to be and you'll attract individuals with the same beliefs, opinions and values. It hard to be fake for too long, the true soul of a person always comes out in time.

In a friendship that ends you will find yourself going through some of the same grief and loss emotions I mentioned in previous chapters of divorce and death of a loved. This type of emotion usually occurs when the friend has wronged you in some way so painful that you never expected it or saw it coming.

In my many years of lasting friendships I have heard some stories that would probably hit home for some. Two best friends for over 10 years.

One is single and one is married. The married friend divorces her husband for cheating and finds out later the woman he is seeing was her best friend all along. These relationships can leave you devastated for a few reasons. The person you shared all of the divorce heart ache with was partly the issue to begin with and now that you discover the person you confided in the most is the person hurting you the most. This friendship will result in a lot of anger and will need time in order to heal.

The friend that tells you everything and appears to have your back supports or simply ignores others talking about you in a negative way. This can be hurtful because you count on your best friends to have your back and shut the negative talk down. You certainly never expect them to befriend the very people trying to hurt you. This friendship may or may not be worthy of saving. It depends on what was said and how willing you are to put your faith back into this relationship.

CHAPTER 15

Empower Women in Fashion

Empowering Women with Fashion

Julie St. Pierre and Bree Armand

Owner & Buyer of Virgo Boutique

Gonzales, LA

As far back as Julie could remember she has always had a passion for fashion and dreamed of what it would be like to one day own her own store. In March of 2008, she decided to stop dreaming, take action and Virgo Boutique was born. In this case the apple doesn't fall far from the tree and her oldest daughter Bree shared in her same passion and love for design. Bree studied Fashion Mechanizing at Louisiana State University so automatically became the buyer for Virgo Boutique where they travel all over the country seeking the best for their clients. It's been over six years since the grand opening and now Virgo is ones of the hottest, most cutting edge Boutiques in Louisiana with their chic and trendy styles in clothing, purses, shoes and accessories. Providing the best in customer service and the latest in fashion this mother daughter team has the best to offer women. Virgo has been featured on reality TV show The Governor's Wife, billboards, newspapers, social media and recently launched their retail online:

www.virgoboutique.com

Visit their store at:

813 E. Ascension St., Gonzales, La. 70737.

Take a Few Tips from the Pros:

1. If You Like It, Buy It. -- If you find something that you believe is truly perfect for you (i.e. it fits perfect, you feel sexy, the price is right) then odds are, you should get it. If it's something you love, then you better bet your bottom dollar that the next girl after you will snag it up in a heartbeat. Get it while you can, and while they have your size. Don't waste your money on the clothes you feel "OK" in. This is completely unacceptable and you don't see Blair Waldorf waltzing around in something that just looks "average," do you?

2. Just because it's Not in Season Now, Doesn't Mean You Shouldn't Buy It. -- Since all of your favorite boutiques are one season ahead of

you, shop smart. Look for those versatile tops that can help you transition from winter to spring. For instance, the top in this post actually has an open back, yet it has long sleeves. This is the perfect transition piece! While it's still winter, pair it with your favorite jacket to help keep warm. Once the warmer weather comes, BAM! The open-back helps keep you cool while STILL looking chic and stylish.

3. Comfy Yet Chic Is the Way to Go. -- If you are on a tight budget, always go for the top that's comfy and chic. Just think about how often you open the doors to your closet only to find out that you don't have that special top that can be dressed up or down. We all need that simple top that you can add jewelry and heels with, or pair it with your favorite pair of jeans and flats. If you're out shopping and you find that comfy and chic top, it should always rank priority over the top that you would only wear for a night out on the town.

As long as you keep these suggestions in mind, you're guaranteed to spend your money and time better

CHAPTER 16

Empower Women with a Makeover

Empowering Women with a Makeover

Kasey Acuff

Professional Make-Up Artist

Memphis, Tennessee

Kasey's professional training begin at the Beauty Institute in Memphis, TN with a focus on aesthetics and then specialized in make-up artistry for brides and their bridal party. She gains respect and sky rocketed her career through her skill and outstanding professional talent. Today, Kasey has helped hundreds of women look their best for all occasions for over 8 years. Her hard work and dedication to beauty encompasses numerous photo shoots for models in print and runway shows. Kasey has been keeping NBA Memphis Grizzlies Girls looking their best for basketball games and in photo shoots since 2010. She has worked with Pepsi and prepped NBA Grizzlies players like Mike Miller and Mike Connelly for commercials as well as being contracted for countless wedding's including that of Zach Randolph's wedding. Kasey has now added her certification in spray tanning to her resume and with her impressive cosmetic bag in tow Kasey has been in high demand traveling hundreds of miles all over the US showcasing her freelance make-up artistry talent so women can look and feel their best.

For more information, /contact:

Kasey.laine@yahoo.com

Instagram: KaseyAcuff

Facebook: www.facebook.com/kaseyacuffmakeupartist

7 Tips from a Pro:

1. Anyone that knows me, knows I'm a huge fan of a good smoky eye. Many women are intimidated just hearing the word smoky, don't be! Smoky eye doesn't always mean dark and harsh, it can be any color you feel comfortable with. The smoky eye gets its name because it looks like smoke, darkest at the bottom and gradually blends into lighter transitional colors. Start with your color choice liner thick at the lash line and blend it all the way into the crease, then take the same color in a shadow and pack it on top of the liner, blend into the crease. Use a tan matte brown in the crease to soften any harsh lines. Finish with a thick coat of mascara and you're done! Practice makes

perfect, once you've mastered this look, I guarantee it will be your favorite look to do!

2. I think we all have struggled with dark circles in our life, if you can remember the color wheel it will be your best friend. For example, if your dark circles have a blueish tone, use an orange tone color corrector under your foundation and it will neutralize the blue. If you have more of a red tone you need to neutralize use a yellow or green tone to conceal. The same colors that neutralize are also complimentary colors for your eyes, blue eyes pop with orange tones, green eyes pop with red tones, and brown eyes pop with lilac.

3. If you're over 50, don't be afraid to experiment with different textures. The taboo saying that you have to only use mattes has never made sense to me, if you only use mattes it can tend to make your skin appear drier and dull. Find a good balance between satin highlight shadows and matte shadows to keep that youthful glow. You should never have all of your shadows shimmery, the colors will all appear as one and you will have no dimension. Always have your blending or contour colors matte, you will get more definition.

4. One of the most requested trends right now has to be contouring. Keep in mind we do not all need to be fully contoured every day. When experimenting with contouring make sure you are enhancing your natural face structure. I always recommend starting with a cream and then setting the cream with the same color in a powder, it will ensure longevity of your look. Also, to avoid the 'muddy' look, try to contour with matte colors and only highlighting with a shimmer.

5. Sometimes, less can be more. Never underestimate the power of a bold lip and lashes. When trying to find your complimentary red lipstick, go to your local makeup counter and try different shades. When trying it find a good, natural looking set of false lashes, make sure the

lashes vary in length, no one's lashes are perfectly symmetrical. My personal favorite is the Demi wispiest.

6. Another trending look right now is the winged liner, or cat eyeliner look. The best advice I can give you is patience and practice while experimenting with this look. Keep your eye open when determining the length and angle of where your wing will start, then you can close your eyes and connect the lines.

7. Last but not least, remember there are technically no rules in makeup, do what makes you feel beautiful and have fun with it! Don't take it so seriously, at the end of the day it all washes off!

CHAPTER 17

Empower Women with Nutrition

Empowering Women with Nutrition

Melissa Stanford

Casting Director for Reality TV/Bravo

New York, NY

Melissa Stanforth is a Casting Director in reality television and is known as a driving force in the industry. Starting her career at the tender age of 19, by the time she graduated college she had already worked for major cable networks such as ABC, NBC, FOX, and Animal Planet just to name a few. She then moved to New York City where her career took off. She worked in the city for a year before picking up and moving to Los Angeles where she continued growing rapidly in her career. She recently relocated back to New York City where she is happily working for Bravo. Coming from the south (Atlanta, GA) and a big Greek family, cooking has always been a huge part of her life. Unlike the typical southern household, Melissa's mother never cooked fried food or anything unhealthy for that matter. They had a huge green house and garden with fresh herbs, spices, and vegetables at their fingertips.

"I grew up in the kitchen, we had sit down dinners every night, and always had big Sunday dinners where everybody came. In our house, mom was always cooking and we always hung out in the kitchen. In fact, some of the best conversations and memories I've had always took place over a good meal or while watching mom cook."

Working and living in the Big Apple is exhausting and when Melissa needs to take a breather you can find her in the kitchen cooking for all of her friends.

"Cooking is my therapy, after living in Atlanta, NYC, and LA, I absolutely love the food culture and have a constant hunger for culinary knowledge and I just can't stop cooking!"

Melissa is working on her first cook book and is looking forward to sharing her culinary journey with the world. Below is a little taste of one of her quick, simple, and healthy recipes.

Recipe: Versatile Bean Salad

(Pairs great with any proteins from grilled fish, chicken, meat or over a bed of kale, it's very versatile, hence the name ;))

Ingredients: (EVERYTHING ORGANIC)

1 can of pinto beans

1 can of black beans

1 can of garbanzo beans

1/2 cup chopped fresh parsley

1 shallot diced

1/2 onion diced

2 tomatoes diced

1-2 cups of blanched broccoli (you can throw it in raw, but blanching gives it that pretty bright green color)

1/2 cup red wine vinegar

Juice from 1 whole lemon (preferably a Meyer)

1/3 cup of good extra virgin olive oil

Salt and pepper to taste (Himalayan salt is best)

Instructions:

Rinse beans in colander first, once dry move to mixing bowl

Mix ingredients over beans

Prep in advance (night before or morning of) for full flavor

Easy and cheap!

CHAPTER 18

Empower Women with Fitness

DeShae Allen Falgoust

Personal Fitness Instructor/Trainer

Prairieville, Louisiana

This 44-year-old mother of 2 beautiful children will tell you fitness is for everyone. Deshae is the perfect example of dedication and fitness. Mother of two Kenedi Leigh 17 years old and Alek Hayes 15 years old, she lives and works in a small town outside of Baton Rouge, Louisiana called Prairieville. She's not all looks either, with a Bachelor of Science degree in Occupational Therapy and spending 25 years in the fitness industry she smart and beautiful inside and out. Deshae has the skill and experience to back up every instruction she gives from being a certified personal trainer & fitness instructor with specialties in Boot camp, Cross Training, Kickboxing, Spin, and Step Aerobics. For 5years she owned and operated her own gym and now currently a contracting trainer & instructor under her own business called: Train 4 L.I.F.E. Which stands for Lifestyle-Inspirational-Fun-Empowering!!

Contact: www.facebook.com/deshae.falgoust

5 Fitness/Workout Tips from a Pro:

1. Be Consistent & Patient! Nothing worth wanting or having comes without persistence & time!

2. Monitor your carb intake! This is definitely one of the best ways to play around with your weight; however, carbohydrates are absolutely essential to your diet, especially if you're an athlete. By reducing your carb intake too much, you could be impairing your performance in the gym.

3. Be creative in your training! Completely switching or changing around your workouts or even adding variety keeps you from getting bored as well as shocks your body producing greater results.

4. Adequate recovery time is a must! You have to have rest days to allow your body to recover and/or adapt.

5. Set realistic goals in small increments and keep track of your progress!

As women, we tend to be perfectionists. We like to make sure we will succeed before we try something, so we avoid the threat of failure and don't reach for new things. This kind of thinking needs to be reversed. We should actually go after the things that scare us.

Be bold and be fearless, so if you do fail, you're able to move on. I've had to learn and I have to continue to remind myself to not dwell on stuff when things don't work out. Emotionally strong females are resilient. It's important to be able to withstand any obstacle. Backing down when the odds are against you is not an option. We all have obstacles, setbacks, pain and disappointments in life. To think you are alone in your pain is never true. I lost my 17-year-old son in an auto accident and he was an absolutely joy in my life. I will never replace that joy but I also know I cannot bring him back. Although my journey in grief is a lifetime I know I have to get up every day and make him proud of his mother just as he was when he was alive. I want to do whatever I can to celebrate his memory which is why the Foundation is so important. Be careful to classify your obstacles as the worst until you've walked a mile in someone else's shoes.

Being strong and independent doesn't mean you have to exclusively rely on yourself. Surrounding yourself with valuable people eases the burden of personal and work related challenges. I tend to call on my Mom, sister, daughter and awesome women friends that I have had for many years so that they can provide good insight and lift me up when I need a boost.

Being sure of yourself also gives you the strength to be supportive for others, and puts you in the right frame of mind to welcome constructive criticism so that you can continue to improve and grow.

Have I not commanded you? Be strong and courageous. Do not be frightened, and do not be dismayed, for the Lord your God is with you wherever you go." Joshua 1:9

My beautiful daughter Kristina Bovia; one of the strongest women I have ever known!

Now stand up…be heard and go make a difference!

For more information, visit:

www.cherierickard.com

Follow on twitter: @cherierickard

Follow on Instagram: iamcherierickard

Facebook: www.facebook.com/authorcherierickard

Purchase books by bulk for your store or organization, schedule speaking events or book signings email:

info@cherierickard.com

ABOUT THE AUTHOR

"Life is a journey that each of us are blessed with at birth. We all will encounter pleasure and pain but what makes us unique is how we transform our pain into power. In 2007 my life would take a turn no mother can even imagine unless you've walked in my shoes. My beautiful 17-year-old son Bryant died tragically in an auto accident coming home one night trying to make curfew. For 7 years I used a pen and paper and later my laptop to write down every pain, struggle and milestone I encountered after the worst day of my life. Facing a cross road in life with depression and destruction versus using my pain and regaining power I chose to live in a way that would honor my son's memory and give glory to God.

I would have never imagined I would become an International Published Author/Speaker/Grief and Empowerment Strategist writing and delivering a powerful message on Building Confidence, overcoming tragedy, grief recovery, making your mess your message and learning to live a life with passion and purpose. It is a message I learned from my own life and one that I use to help others apply to their own lives".

[signature: Cherie Rickard]

STEP IN TO YOUR PURPOSE

Cherie's award-winning book, ***Wake-Up Call...A Mother's Grief Journey***, is a true story written after her 17-year-old son that was killed tragically in an auto accident. Cherie's widely recognized 2nd book, ***Healing Your Wounded Spirit*** hit #1 on Amazon in Love & Loss and gives guidance and support others need after divorce, death of a loved-one and broken friendships. She delivers a stimulating message based on her 3rd book ***Strong Women*** which will not only guide you but show you how to improve your life through boosted confidence, interviewing skills, self-esteem and independence. Cherie's new book, ***How to Live a Life with Passion & Purpose*** will not only push you into action but show you how to take action in life to get what you want and deserve.

Cherie frequently appears as a featured guest and expert on numerous Broadcast & Podcast radio programs and is a speaker & mentor. Cherie has been featured in Publishers Weekly, awarded special recognition through several Book Awards and has had numerous articles published on other websites and social media. She is a motivational speaker to a wide variety of audiences; including business and networking organizations, social and charitable organizations, students (ranging from high school to college), women's organizations, business development, self-publishing and authors as well as the healthcare, hospice and bereavement industries.

Cherie's skills and experience expands with over 20 years in the Healthcare industry as a Registered Nurse, Medical Professional, Business development, marketing specialist, Grief & Empowerment Strategist. She is a member of the Women Speakers Association and E-women Network.

Her powerful and passionate message educates, inspires, motivates, teaches and offers practical guidance to those who have experienced any kind of tragedy, set back or challenge in their lives. Her new YouTube Channel "Step into Your Purpose" launched February 2017.

CPSIA information can be obtained
at www.ICGtesting.com
Printed in the USA
LVOW05s1530060817
544024LV00015B/1280/P